LET'S TALK SEX

LET'S TALK SEX

The no-nonsense guide to sex education

DAVINA McCALL & ANITA NAIK

Books

TRANSWORLD PUBLISHERS
61–63 Uxbridge Road, London W5 5SA
a division of The Random House Group Ltd

RANDOM HOUSE AUSTRALIA (PTY) LTD
20 Alfred Street, Milsons Point, Sydney,
New South Wales 2061, Australia

RANDOM HOUSE NEW ZEALAND LTD
18 Poland Road, Glenfield, Auckland 10, New Zealand

RANDOM HOUSE SOUTH AFRICA (PTY) LTD
Isle of Houghton, Corner of Boundary Road & Carse O'Gowrie,
Houghton 2198, South Africa

Let's Talk Sex is produced by betty for Channel 4

Published 2007 by Channel 4 Books
a division of Transworld Publishers

Text copyright © Davina McCall and betty 2007

A catalogue record for this book is available from the British Library.

ISBN 9781905026180

Designed, illustrated and typeset by Julia Lloyd.

Printed in Great Britain by Clays Ltd, Bungay, Suffolk

1 3 5 7 9 10 8 6 4 2

Papers used by Transworld Publishers are natural, recyclable products made from
wood grown in sustainable forests. The manufacturing processes conform
to the environmental regulations of the country of origin.

Davina McCall was bought up in Surrey. She worked as a waitress in Paris and a model agent in London and even had a short-lived singing career before deciding her real passion is presenting. She landed her first job for MTV in 1992 and has since gone on to present a number of hit TV shows including *Big Brother*, *StreetMate*, the *Brits* and the *BAFTAs*. As a mother of three young children Davina doesn't profess to be an expert on sex education but she has been on a journey of discovery during *Let's Talk Sex*. She hopes that this book and the accompanying series will help Britain's parents open up the lines of communication and give their children the information they need to make informed choices and lead a happy, healthy life.

Anita Naik is an author and journalist. She started her career as the agony aunt of *Just 17* magazine and has since talked to teens and parents about everything from sex and body worries to relationship problems in *B*, *More*, *Closer* and *TV Quick* magazines. She is also the author of over 30 books, 17 of which are for the 10–14 year old teenage market and cover everything from sex education to personal safety and fitness. Anita is the mother of a six-month-old baby girl. For more information visit www.anitanaik.co.uk

Contents

Acknowledgements

I will never forget the journey I have travelled whilst making this TV series and researching this book. I have met so many amazing people and I would like to say a massive thank you to them all, particularly: Dionne, Sam and baby Hope; Kerry-Ann, Stephanie and Danny; Rory, James, Steven and Femi; Kerry and Leanne; Anna Martinez from the Sex Education Forum; Dr Colm O'Mahony, GUM clinic consultant; Sanderijn van der Doef; Dr Ann McPherson; school nurse Viv Crouch; Dave Harris and the pupils, staff and parents at Serlby Park School; Ralph Jaggar and the pupils, staff and parents at Acton Pastures Primary School; and finally Ian Carré, Suzanne Lynch and Liz Warner at betty.

Without you all, this project would not have been possible.

Anita Naik would like to thank:
Naomi Templeton, Jenni Baxter, Matt Whyman and Charlotte Owen for advice, research and parental stories.

Introduction

THIS MAY SOUND LIKE A BOLD STATEMENT, BUT I BELIEVE THIS book is one that no parent should be without. As well as my new baby boy, I've got two little girls and my dilemmas started with their births. What do I call their private parts? Noony? Front bottom? Flower? Surely not vagina? Every time I said that word I'd go red. But, why not vagina? What's wrong with the word? Well, I grew up embarrassed to say it, as did most of my girlfriends, so is it any wonder that we British have got it so wrong when it comes to talking about sex and relationships with our kids?

Recently my five-year-old asked me how she got in my tummy and, boy, did that throw me. What was I supposed to say? I knew I wanted to tell her the truth, but I was stuck for how much information I should impart and in what words. I did some research and finally told her that Daddy had planted a seed in my tummy and she had grown from that. Thankfully that seemed to do the trick, but my worry then was, for how long will this be enough and, if I'm finding this hard now, surely it's only going to get worse.

Do I wait to discuss sex when they ask me about it, or do I talk to them before that point? Worse still, how do I get them to feel comfortable enough that they would even dream of coming to talk to me? And my biggest fear – what if I talk to them and that makes them want to go out and sleep with someone faster than they would have done if I'd kept quiet? So what would you do if your thirteen-year-old daughter came home and said her best friend was having sex with her boyfriend? My natural reaction would have been to be completely shocked and to do everything in my power to try to distance my daughter from her friend – but then through talking to experts I realized that all that would do would be to send out a clear message to my daughter that she can't talk to me about sex without having me freak out, and that would be a travesty.

So the answer to all the above parental angst is this – foster an environment at home where your children feel that they can talk to you (I know – that's quite hard in itself, but read the book and all will become clear), because then you'll know that in a crisis your kids will come to you, whatever that crisis may be. A non-judgemental and unconditional approach is the way forward – bloody hard, but possible. Then try to get your teenagers to formulate their own opinions. How do they feel about sex? How do they feel about their friends' behaviour? Challenge them to back up their ideas, find out how their minds are working and, most importantly, listen. If teenagers have formulated their own views and moral standpoint on something they are much more likely to adhere to the boundaries they have set themselves than to your views and morals, which have been forced upon them. The mad thing is that, given the space to discover their own minds, many will adopt a similar viewpoint to you anyway!

Lastly, when it comes to making the right decisions concerning sex and relationships, there is one vital ingredient that you can't afford to miss out on with your kids – self-esteem. Some of the teenagers that I met while making this TV series had bucketloads of it and because of that they had a great attitude to sex – they were waiting until they were ready to have sex, and when they did they were in loving relationships.

When it comes to talking about sex and relationships, this book will map out age-specific topics and show you how to cover them appropriately and sensitively. Remember, it doesn't have to be a nightmare if we don't make it one. I have learnt so much working on the programmes and this book that, far from dreading the whole process of talking to my kids about sex, I now feel confident and empowered.

Talk talk talk talk talk – that's what I say! And good luck!

PS Your teenagers may still make mistakes in life, but at least you'll be the ones they turn to when they do!

Some sections of this book are written specifically for your children. These are labelled 'Parent-free zones'.

1

SEX AND RELATIONSHIP EDUCATION – WHAT'S IT ALL ABOUT?

YOU'VE LIVED THROUGH TWO-HOURLY FEEDS, ENDLESS TODDLER tantrums and the 'I'm not going to school' blues, so why does the idea of your son or daughter turning into a teenager cause you so much anxiety? The chances are that sex, relationships and puberty have much to do with it – and who can blame you for worrying, with the papers full of stories of underage pregnancies and rising sexually transmitted infection (STI) levels amongst teenagers. The good news is, most children won't turn into hoodies with ASBOs trailing in their wake and, while we do have a high teenage pregnancy rate, studies show that when given the right information, kids make sensible and well-thought-out decisions about sex.

On the whole, having met a load of young people for these programmes, I think teenagers get a really bad press these days. In reality, most are sensible and clever, with a deep interest in what's fair and right. They understand more than we give them credit for and really just want to suck up as much information as possible about life, sex and relationships – so why on earth aren't we helping them?

One reason is probably the way we all got our sex education, which in my days consisted of a fairly inept look at how babies were made, what to do to stop them being made, and what might happen if you made one – all rolled together in one lesson, with grainy video of someone giving birth thrown in! These days, while sex education is now known as sex and relationship education (SRE), it's still patchy and, because it's not compulsory in the UK, no-one's guaranteed to get any. If your kids are lucky they might get some information about the nuts and bolts of sex, alongside some facts about contraception and sexually transmitted infections, but only the extremely lucky also get the relationship education which, let's face it, is the bit that will help them to delay sex and boost their self-esteem, confidence and body image.

As the mother of two girls and a boy I'm the first to admit that I've been as guilty as the rest in believing that talking about sex at an early age is a bad thing, just making our children curious to do it and eager to rip their clothes off and get out there. But my eyes have been opened, thanks mainly to Anna Martinez from the Sex Education Forum, genito-urinary medicine (GUM) consultant Dr Colm O'Mahony and Dutch sexologist Sanderijn van der Doef, not to mention the many teenagers, parents and experts I spoke to both here and in Holland. But I do appreciate that it's hard to talk to your kids about sex, especially when no-one's ever talked to you about it. I certainly am not going to be holier than thou about what's right and what's wrong, because this subject has been a personal journey for me as well.

What's surprised me on this television series is that, time and time again, my own beliefs have been challenged, sometimes in a close-to-the-knuckle way and other times in an enlightening way. For me one of the most eye-opening conversations was with a mum called Kerry-Ann who has talked openly and incredibly frankly to her daughter Stephanie about sex since Stephanie was young. As a result, Stephanie is a smart and savvy young woman who is very sexually aware at fifteen. Personally, I'm not sure I am quite ready for Kerry-Ann's full-on approach and technique, but being frank and open definitely works.

By far the most enlightening part of the journey for me was my trip to Holland, where I watched several utterly fantastic classes on sex and relationships and realized just why it is that the Dutch have one of the lowest rates of teenage pregnancy in the world. To say it was a lightbulb moment is an understatement, because over there I watched a group of eleven-year-old kids being taught not only about sex but also, more importantly, about how to deal with relationships and peer pressure, and also how to take care of themselves and each other. These kids were brilliant: not only could they talk about safe sex and condoms, but also about different kinds of love and why it is important to wait until you're ready to have sex. Because of this early sex and relationship education in schools and within the home, there is a greater openness about sex in Holland and, as a direct result of this, improved sexual health among young people.

By comparison, fifteen-year-old girls in England are lucky if they receive ten SRE lessons at school and as a result are twice as likely to be sexually active as those in Holland. The reason for this is that sex and relationship education in the UK is incredibly patchy and lopsided: while the biological facts are compulsory under the National Curriculum, SRE is only advised within Personal, Social and Health Education (PSHE) lessons. This means schools can opt out of teaching it, parents can take their children out of it and SRE can be limited to a very small part of the PSHE curriculum. The relationship part often falls by the wayside and/or is taught by a teacher who gets lumbered with it. Surveys show that 41 per cent of British girls think their sex education was too little, too late, with another 16 per cent saying the teacher was too embarrassed for the lessons to be useful. And this is exactly why we end up with teenagers who can describe how two cells come together to make a baby, but don't know how to use contraception, protect themselves from STIs, or stand up to a partner by saying no to sex.

The annoying thing is, we know sex education works. A study from the London School of Hygiene and Tropical Medicine found that girls who have more than ten sex education sessions are less likely to get pregnant, while boys who have more than ten sessions are more likely to use condoms. Sadly, only a third of the young people questioned had had more than ten lessons. New government guidance from the Qualification and Curriculum Authority (QCA), issued in November 2005, does aim to redress this imbalance, with a great strategy focusing on families, puberty and physical changes, as well as on friendships and how to make 'healthy' choices when it comes to sex – but it doesn't take a genius to see that until sex and relationship education is made compulsory in schools nothing is going to change.

Of course, you may be thinking, 'Where do I come in?' Well, as a parent you have more of an impact on your kids' sex lives than you might think. Studies show that open and honest sex and relationship education that starts in the home and at a young age (that's right from when your children notice that your naked body is different to theirs) really works – it works as in helping your kids to delay sex until they're ready; works as in helping your kids to practise safe sex; and works as in helping your kids have a healthy and positive view of relationships. Plus it doesn't matter if you didn't get much sex education yourself, or if you have no idea where to start, or even if you feel excruciatingly embarrassed about bringing the subject up. Sex and relationship education can be done very successfully and that's what this book is all about. Read it, share the information with your children, or even leave it out for them to peruse at their leisure and, believe me, your kids will thank you for ever.

SEXUAL KNOWLEDGE VERSUS INNOCENCE

'I find it shocking that parents and schools haven't adapted enough to how society has changed and haven't responded to the needs of kids. The exposure level with sex was a lot lower when most of us were younger... These days you can't leave it to chance, or else your kids won't be prepared and may well become sexually active before they are ready because they hold the wrong expectations of sex and what it can do for you.'

ANNA MARTINEZ, Sex Education Forum

Before I go on, I want to say a word about the fight to keep our children innocent and the belief that talking about sex makes them eager to get naked and jump into bed with the first available person. Trust me when I say that I know talking honestly about sex and love won't have your kids giving blow jobs behind the bike sheds, or rushing to clinics to get the pill on their twelfth birthdays. This used to be my belief until I met and spoke to a number of parents and teenagers and realized that whether we like it or not, we can't stop our kids finding out about sex so it pays to be open about it. Take Kerry-Ann, who says, 'My daughter Stephanie came home when she was eight and asked me what a blow job was and I honestly just nearly dropped dead on the floor. I thought, that's it – I've got to teach her about sex properly at home. I grew up hearing sex was cool but didn't get any details so I thought, bloody hell, this must be the most exciting thing on the planet, I'm going to try that and it was the worst mistake of my life. I didn't want my daughter to go through the same thing.'

As you can see, keeping quiet about sex doesn't keep our kids innocent, because all that happens is they end up making up their own minds about it by listening to all the information that can be picked up in the school playground, on TV and around them in general. And let's face it, today even young children are surrounded by sexual images – from steamy TV shows to raunchy lyrics and sexed-up advertising campaigns. If you don't discuss what they're seeing and hearing, they won't be able to tell the difference between myth and fact and won't be able to make the right decisions for themselves.

Just take a look at the statistics. In the UK around 42,000 girls under eighteen get pregnant every year. Of these, around

8,000 are under sixteen (the highest rate in Europe). On top of this, a new poll suggests that around 20 per cent of young people under sixteen have sex, and the younger they are, the less likely they are to use contraception or have safe sex. None of this is due to our enlightened and liberal approach to sex, but the very opposite. This is why young people need to hear your views. It's hard to understand love and commitment, face peer pressure, and feel good about changing bodies if you have no-one to tell your deepest, darkest fears to. And trust me, your children won't be able to do this at school, or with friends or with partners if they can't first do it with you.

Plus – and this is a big PLUS – your kids are eager to know about sex and love, because one day soon it will be the main-stay of their conversations, whether you like it or not. Make falling in love and sex something secretive and they'll just become more curious and eager to discover the real truth they'll feel you're hiding from them. Demystify it for them and they'll have a more level-headed attitude that won't have them falling for the first pick-up line thrown their way.

What are your children learning from you?

'My mum and nan told me I had to protect myself as sperm can make babies when I was about thirteen, so I tried the pill. I stopped taking it because of my irregular periods but I didn't understand there was more than one pill I could try so I didn't use anything – I just didn't think pregnancy could happen so quickly.'

DIONNE, 16

The other problem with not talking to your children directly about sex and relationships is that they will still pick up messages, attitudes and information from the way you behave. The bad news is these may not be the attitudes you want them to have. For instance, if you're watching TV and flick channels or bury your head in a newspaper every time sex comes on the screen, they'll believe sex is something to be embarrassed about and something you can't handle talking to them about. If your child mentions that someone at school is pregnant/has a love bite/was caught kissing and you make harsh comments or use it as a way to warn your kids to stay clear of sex, they'll learn that you're not someone they can come to when they are confused or in trouble.

These may well be off-the-cuff responses or just comments you don't really mean, but if you don't back them up with chats about why you feel the way you do or regularly bring up the topic of relationships and sex, your teenagers will simply make their own assumptions about what you're able to talk to them about and what you're not. Shocked as you may be by what they tell you and what happens around you, it's better to use these everyday instances as a way in to talk about sex and relationships. This way you can still tell them how you feel, but make it a two-way conversation that allows you to see what they know, and what they need to know.

'Sex education is so bad in the UK because the British have a reticence about discussing sex and there has never been much support for proper sex education either from parents, schools or the government. So as long as it's not obligatory, it just won't happen. Some schools have taken

it on themselves to get it right and do employ people to come in and help with sex and relationship education. For example, in our area, one of our health advisers used to go into schools and at least start the process, and the teachers greatly appreciated this. However, we had to stop this recently because of the huge demand on the sexual health service itself and we couldn't spare a health adviser to do this work any more. To improve sex and relationship education, legislation is needed to make it a statutory duty for schools to teach it competently. I think schools will probably even like this, because then parents can be told that this has to be done and the risk of parental complaints is greatly reduced.'

DR COLM O'MAHONY, MD, FRCP, BSc., Dip.Ven.,
Consultant in Genito-urinary Medicine

When should sex education start?

'I started having conversations with my mum about sex early when I started asking questions. You hear things in the playground and you hear friends talking about something and I would ask mum and she would tell me in a basic way. I've been talking to her ever since – she found it difficult but she would rather I learnt from her than someone I don't trust. And she tells me the emotional side rather than this goes here, and that gets me more involved and makes it easier to understand.'

STEPHANIE, 15

*'I lost my virginity when I was twelve – I didn't use pro-
tection and I really regretted it and felt ashamed. I didn't
get sex education until I was thirteen and haven't had any
since then. I can't remember what it was about – all I can
remember is we got a little green packet with sanitary
towels and leaflets in. I think that's poor.'*

KERRY, 16

*'I've been playing about in the park with girls since I was
twelve. I didn't learn about sex in school and didn't have
a clue what I was doing. I learnt about sex and what to
do through my mates. The only education I got from
school was a blow job in the toilets. They should teach it
at a younger age rather than not wanting people to know
about it until they're older.'*

RORY, 18

Sex education that works starts early. That's as soon as your
children start asking questions and as soon as they start getting
inquisitive about bodies and babies. I know many people will
gasp at the idea of beginning sex education so young, but I'm
not talking the mechanics of sex, more the issues around sex
and relationships, such as facts about the body, talks about
love, friendships and, as they get older, confidence issues and
self-esteem.

Also bear in mind that mentioning sex or something sexual
doesn't always mean your kids want to know all about the
plumbing bits. In many cases, questions from younger children
come from a point of confusion, which means you need to
work out where they are emotionally and developmentally

before you answer them. A good way to do this is simply to ask where they heard a term and what they think it might mean.

Tempting as it is to brush the more embarrassing questions under the carpet for when they're older, it's important not to delay giving information. One reason for this is that puberty is happening earlier than ever. Girls, on average, now start their periods at the age of twelve, eight months sooner than thirty years ago, and this is just an average, meaning many girls start even younger, at around nine or ten. Another reason is that providing basic and age-appropriate responses – i.e. in terms of what they can understand – when your children are young helps make your job smoother because it provides a platform on which you can add more knowledge over time, making it easier on you and easier on your kids. For instance, the parent who talks about body parts, love and where babies come from to a curious five-year-old is the parent who will more easily be able to talk about delaying sex and using contraception to an eleven-year-old.

Of course it is difficult to know when to raise issues, so it's best to work around your time-frame and that of your children. Kids will usually tell you when something is on their mind; if they don't, try to watch the TV programmes they're watching to see what they might be picking up and what needs to be discussed. However, the most important thing is to give them opportunities to ask questions, again from an early age. This means being proactive in starting conversations about sex and relationships from as early as possible. Young children, for instance, notice everything from pregnant bellies to naked bodies and this is an ideal starting place to talk about the differences between boys and girls, and how babies end up in tummies. Remember, we're talking age-appropriate information: all your toddler is looking for is very basic information, not the whole shebang.

Who should provide sex education?

Mums or dads – that's the question. In most households children will choose the parent they feel most comfortable talking to and thereby make your job easier, and in many cases it is the mum. However, fathers can also play a vital role with both sons and daughters by backing up what mum says and being an extra resource to come to with questions about relationships as well as sex.

If you're a single parent it's more than possible to do a good job. Single fathers of daughters in particular shouldn't despair: like any other parent, if you start early, the later, more difficult stuff is easier to bring up and discuss (see Chapter 2). Plus, if you give your daughter the option of speaking to other women if she is embarrassed (if there is no-one in your family, try one of the helplines in the Resources section), she'll still use you as her main point of reference.

If you don't get on with your kids, talking about sex and relationships can of course be a potential minefield and a battle of wills. If so, you need to look at how you communicate with each other before talking about sex. Do you listen as much as you speak? Do your children trust you? What would improve your relationship? (They can enlighten you here if you're willing to listen.) Sex and relationship discussions should not be about laying down the law, telling them what will happen if they get pregnant/get someone pregnant and emphasizing the doom and gloom aspect. Talks need to be a conversation (especially with older kids) that allows for a difference of opinion and for real discussion to happen.

It can help to remember that the scenarios your teenagers discuss with you may not be things they are actually going through but potential worries, things they have witnessed or simply the worst-case possibility going through their head. Getting into a wild panic and assuming they are having sex because they have mentioned it won't help your child, and won't help you feel reassured. Listen to what they're saying and they'll listen to you (even if they look as if they're not).

What if I've left it too late?

It's never too late to talk about sex and relationships, and while starting early helps make it easier on both of you, it is more than possible to reach a teenager stuck in his or her tunnel (my word for how teenagers shut themselves off from the world at puberty). A good way to do so is to talk to them about love and relationships first, then when they feel comfortable move on to sex.

The difference between teenagers and other age groups is that they have more assumptions that need to be discussed and challenged, and their experience may outweigh their actual knowledge. Again, ways into talking to your kids are the comments they make, the TV programmes you watch together, their magazines and even what's going on at home. Depending on your child, you can take the softly, softly approach and first try to uncover what they know, then what they want to know; or you can adopt the tough love approach and openly suggest that a few conversations about sex wouldn't go amiss.

Even if you know your son or daughter has had sex, it doesn't mean that it's too late. I know from talking to teenagers who are having sex that many of them regret their first time but then don't know how to turn down sex again, or don't understand how to use contraception effectively or even how sexually transmitted infections are passed. So, hard as it is to accept, bear in mind that a sexually active teenager needs your help and support even more.

What to talk about

'I'm strong because my mum brought me up this way. I don't take anything from lads or girls. I have a protective bubble that keeps me safe that my mum built up and it gives me faith and makes me think, hang on, I don't want to do this. I also know most people have trouble saying no, but if I get into a situation I know how to say no.'

STEPHANIE, 15

Besides passing on basic facts and information about sex and relationships, you also need to give your children relationship and life skills. That is, ways they can learn to communicate, listen, negotiate their relationships and ways they can feel good about themselves and their bodies so that they're not at the mercy of people with stronger personalities. To help get your kids to trust your view rather than assume you know nothing, it's important to be honest with them as soon as the subject arises. Answer the inquisitive questions about you and your partner, about what those semi-naked people are doing on TV, and what certain words mean, and they'll believe you when you start talking about delaying sex. Discussion can also be sparked anywhere and at any time. Think about commenting on something that is happening within the family in order to generate chat and a conversation about relationships. Finally, bear in mind that sex and relationship education in the home also tends to take place over a long time, and there may well be periods when your kids seem reluctant to talk and just roll their eyes at you, but persevere. If you can get them to view sex and relationship talks within your home as an ongoing conversation, they'll feel able to raise more personal and anxiety-ridden issues with you, rather than suffer alone.

This is one of the huge pros of home sex and relationship education compared to SRE at school. In school the pressure amongst kids to make light of what's being taught is huge, and very rarely are issues personalized, which means many fears remain unspoken. Try to find out what your children are being taught at school, then you can reiterate these same subjects at home and give your kids the space to talk about their own views and what may or may not be troubling them.

Below are some of the most important things to remember when talking about sex and relationships (for more specific information on these, see Chapters 2 and 3).

Admit that sex is good and normal

If you cast sex as something negative and bad, your kids won't believe you because there are too many other sources around saying the opposite. Then they'll either ignore what you say and try to prove you wrong, or they'll simply grow up being afraid and anxious about something that's natural and normal in the right circumstances.

Talk to boys as much as girls

Talking about sex is easier with girls because you can start with periods and breasts, and as many mature quicker you'll be able to have frank discussions earlier. Some parents also feel girls need to have information about puberty and sex more than boys do because they are more vulnerable, but to be fully informed all teenagers need to know about sex and puberty and how it affects both sexes. And don't fool yourself: sex and puberty are as frightening and alarming to boys as they are to girls, and boys are just as vulnerable to peer pressure as girls are, perhaps even more so thanks to teen male bravado.

Link sex to emotions

If you feel nervous about discussing sex with your children, it can be easy just to stick to the facts – i.e. this is how to avoid having a baby, this is how to use a condom, and here's how to say no! However, in order for your kids really to be able to put what you're teaching them into practice, you need to talk about how sex, though physical, always has emotional consequences. Topics to discuss in addition to the facts are their beliefs and expectations, morals, attitudes and responsibilities.

Don't be afraid to tell your kids what you think

While it's important to try to give your teenagers the chance to create their own opinions, don't be afraid to tell them what you think. For one thing, they'll already know if you hold strong religious and/or cultural values about sex and relationships;

and they'll want you to be honest (even if they later choose to believe something else).

Focus on self-esteem

Self-esteem is not just some American buzzword but the key to a healthy attitude to sex. If your kids feel that they are rubbish at everything, unattractive, too fat or too thin and not as clever, witty or charming as everyone else, then they're more likely to do things to be accepted and loved. This is because low self-esteem makes you question your ability to make good decisions, and leaves you unable to stand up to someone with a stronger personality. This means you're more likely to be persuaded/manipulated into sex, or that you will try to value yourself through sex. The way out of this is to get your child to hone their individual talents and strengths to see their worth, as well as to talk to them about esteem and confidence. Good self-esteem will help your children to:

- Delay sex until they are ready – because they'll feel strong enough to do what they believe is right for themselves.
- Feel good about themselves – so they won't think they have to make someone love them through sex.
- Know that they deserve a good partner and a good relationship.

It's therefore important to know that how you talk to your children will affect their self-esteem. Constant criticizing, labelling and blaming will deplete your child's self-esteem and lead them to have negative feelings about themselves. While I am not suggesting you never snap at your child again, nor reprimand them, bear in mind that balancing this with praise and appreciation is an important way to build self-esteem. And remember, if you want to help your kids to feel good about themselves, you need to start with yourself, as your children will pick up messages about self-esteem from how you act and talk about yourself.

Be someone your kids want to talk to

Finally, try not to panic about sex and relationship education. While there is a lot to get through, you can do it and it can be a bonding experience for both of you. Remember, you don't have to be po-faced about sex. Try to have a bit of a laugh, talk about it in a relaxed way and, above all, be yourself. This way you'll seem credible to your kids. Ways to convince them that you're worthy are:

- Avoid judgements. Hard as it is, silence the preacher in you. You may just want to keep them safe, but they'll read it as you trying to control their lives.
- Be genuine. Your children know you. Fake it, bluff it or pretend you understand when actually you're silently raging inside and they'll know you're not being honest with them.
- Make time for them. In a busy and manic world, it's likely that your kids' time-frames may not be your time-frame, but try to answer questions as they come up rather than saying 'We'll talk later', because later may be too late. This doesn't mean everything has to be dropped when the topic of sex comes up, but more that

an immediate question needs to be answered, while discussion can be delayed until later.

- Don't overreact. Avoid going too far either way. Thanking them profusely for coming to you with a problem will turn them off, as will getting angry over a subject you feel strongly about. Regardless of how thrilled or shocked you are, bite the bullet, relax and try to go with the flow.

THE SEX QUIZ

HOW MUCH DO YOU REALLY KNOW ABOUT SEX?

Before you start talking to your kids about sex and relationships it pays to know how sound your own knowledge is. Try the sex quiz below: it will help you to determine your own sexual knowledge and that of your children. Answers on page 35.

1. At what age do boys generally begin puberty?
   a. Age 9
   b. Age 10
   c. Age 11
   d. Age 12

2. At what age do girls generally begin puberty?
   a. Age 9
   b. Age 10
   c. Age 11
   d. Age 12

3. When a girl begins puberty, how will she usually start developing?
   a. Onset of periods
   b. Onset of breast growth
   c. Onset of body hair growth
   d. Onset of body odour
   e. All of the above

4. When does a girl generally begin her periods?
   a. When she's 10
   b. When she begins masturbating
   c. When she reaches 48kg (7½ stone)
   d. When she's ready to have sex

5. Generally, what are the first changes to occur to a boy when he reaches puberty?
   a. His genitals start to grow
   b. He begins to sweat more
   c. He starts to get body hair
   d. He grows much taller
   e. All of the above

6. How many times larger do a boy's testicles become during puberty?
   a. Approximately three times larger
   b. Approximately four times larger
   c. Approximately seven times larger
   d. Approximately ten times larger

7. Which is the sexiest part of your body?
   a. Your genitals
   b. Your brain
   c. Your neck
   d. Your mouth

8. What is the speed of sperm when it leaves the end of a man's penis during ejaculation?
   a. 5 mph
   b. 13 mph
   c. 28 mph
   d. 39 mph

9. How many sperm are contained in an average ejaculation?
   a. 1,000
   b. 10,000
   c. 1 million
   d. 100 million

10. How many sperm are needed to fertilize a woman's egg so that she gets pregnant?
   a. 1
   b. 5
   c. 10
   d. 100

11. What is the legal age of consent for sexual intercourse in the UK?
    a. 15
    b. 16
    c. 17
    d. There is no age of consent

12. What is the legal age of consent for gay sex in the UK?
    a. 16
    b. 17
    c. 18
    d. There isn't one

13. What is the legal age of consent for lesbian sex in the UK?
    a. 16
    b. 17
    c. 18
    d. There isn't one

14. On average, how many times do single males masturbate?
    a. Two or three times a week
    b. Four or five times a week
    c. Six or seven times a week
    d. More than seven times a week

15. On average, how many times do single females masturbate?
    a. Two or three times a month
    b. Four or five times a month
    c. Six or seven times a month
    d. More than seven times a month

16. In the UK, how many girls under the age of 16 have had sex?
    a. 1 in 3
    b. 1 in 5
    c. 1 in 10
    d. 1 in 18

17. What is the risk of a young woman getting pregnant if she has unprotected sexual intercourse 14 days before her next period?
    a. 10 per cent
    b. 30 per cent
    c. 50 per cent
    d. 90 per cent

18. Can you get pregnant during your period?
    a. Yes
    b. No

19. Can you get pregnant if the man doesn't have an orgasm?
    a. Yes
    b. No

20. Can a girl get pregnant before she starts her periods?
    a. Yes
    b. No

21. Can a woman get pregnant if the man doesn't actually put his penis inside her?
    a. Yes
    b. No

22. Can you get pregnant if the man withdraws before he ejaculates?
    a. Yes
    b. No

23. Which country has the highest teenage pregnancy rate?
    a. France
    b. Holland
    c. The UK
    d. The USA

24. How long can the average sperm hang around in the average vagina?
    a. Less than 4 hours
    b. Less than 12 hours
    c. Less than 36 hours
    d. More than 5 days

25. What do condoms help to protect against?
    a. Getting pregnant
    b. Chlamydia
    c. HIV
    d. Gonorrhoea
    e. All of the above

26. How long after having sexual intercourse is the emergency contraceptive pill (morning after pill) effective?
    a. 24 hours
    b. 48 hours
    c. 72 hours
    d. 5 days

27. How many times a year can a woman have the emergency contraceptive pill?
    a. Once
    b. Twice
    c. Three times
    d. More than four times

28. Where can a woman get the emergency contraceptive pill?
    a. A chemist
    b. Her GP
    c. A Brook clinic
    d. Any sexual health drop-in centre
    e. All of the above

29. The emergency contraceptive pill is most effective if taken within 24 hours, but how effective?
    a. 50 per cent
    b. 75 per cent
    c. 95 per cent
    d. 100 per cent

30. How effective is the contraceptive pill if taken as instructed?
    a. Nearly 50 per cent
    b. Nearly 70 per cent
    c. Nearly 90 per cent
    d. Nearly 100 per cent

31. What does STI stand for?

    . . . .

32. Name three STIs
    1. . . . .
    2. . . . .
    3. . . . .

33. The best precaution against catching or passing on an STI is to:
    a. Withdraw before ejaculation
    b. Ensure the woman is on the pill
    c. Use a condom
    d. Sleep with only one person

34. Which of the following are signs that you might have an STI?
    a. A smelly, coloured discharge from your penis or vagina
    b. Pain when peeing
    c. Warty lumps on your penis or around your vagina
    d. An itchy sore penis or vagina
    e. All of the above

35. Can you catch an STI from a lavatory seat?
    a. Yes
    b. No

36. Can you get an STI from oral sex?
    a. Yes
    b. No

37. Do you always know when you've got a sexually transmitted infection?
    a. Yes
    b. No

38. How many 16–25-year-old women have chlamydia?
    a. 1 in 5
    b. 1 in 10
    c. 1 in 15
    d. 1 in 20

39. If you've got chlamydia, what symptoms might you have?
   a. Genital discharge
   b. Cystitis (painful and frequent peeing)
   c. No symptoms at all
   d. Pain
   e. All of the above

40. For women, what is the possible long-term effect of contracting chlamydia?
   a. Infertility
   b. Vaginal discharge
   c. Pain when having sex
   d. Chronic pelvic pain
   e. All of the above

41. What is the name of the virus that causes AIDS?

. . . .

42. If a man has one-off unprotected sexual intercourse with a woman who is HIV+, what are the chances of his catching the virus?
   a. 1 in 5
   b. 1 in 20
   c. 1 in 100
   d. 1 in 1,000

43. What is the most common STI in the UK?
    a. Chlamydia
    b. Gonorrhoea
    c. Genital herpes
    d. HIV

44. Where can a woman go to get a referral for an abortion?
    a. Her GP
    b. Her local drop-in clinic
    c. The British Pregnancy Advisory Service
    d. Marie Stopes International
    e. All of the above

45. What is the legal limit for an abortion?
    a. Up to 18 weeks
    b. Up to 20 weeks
    c. Up to 22 weeks
    d. Up to 24 weeks

46. Can a woman get an abortion free on the NHS?
    a. Yes
    b. No
    c. Depends on your circumstances
    d. Depends on how pregnant you are

47. What is the single most common risk when having an abortion?
    a. Risk of infertility
    b. Risk of infection
    c. Risk of blood loss
    d. Risk of loss of sensation when having sex

ANSWERS

1. At what age do boys generally begin puberty?
   d. Age 12
   Boys tend to start around two years after girls – see Chapter 3 for more on this.

2. At what age do girls generally begin puberty?
   b. Age 10
   Though many girls are now starting puberty younger than this – see Chapter 3 for more on this.

3. When a girl begins puberty, how will she usually start developing?
   b. Onset of breast growth
   Approximately 80–85 per cent of the time, puberty starts with breast growth (in the other 15–20 per cent of cases the first sign may be long, coarse hair in the pubic area) and girls may notice small, tender lumps under one or both nipples that will get bigger over the next few years. When breasts first begin to develop, it is not unusual for one breast to be larger than the other. However, as they develop, they will most likely even out before they reach their final size and shape.

4. **When does a girl generally begin her periods?**
    c. When she reaches 48kg (7½ stone)
    Gaining weight is a normal part of puberty and the increase in body fat is essential for oestrogen production to start. However, if you are concerned about a weight increase, or if your daughter is, talk it over with your doctor to see if your child is in the right weight percentile.

5. **Generally, what are the first changes to occur to a boy when he reaches puberty?**
    a. His genitals start to grow
    This may not be easily noticed when it first begins, but shortly afterwards a boy will begin to see the growth of pubic hair. Growth of the penis generally begins after this has appeared; after which your son may experience more erections due to an increase in sex hormones.

6. **How many times larger do a boy's testicles become during puberty?**
    c. Approximately seven times larger
    The first enlargement of the testicles occurs almost at the same time as the appearance of pubic hair.

7. **Which is the sexiest part of your body?**
    b. Your brain
    It's here that everything starts – feelings, sensations, hormonal releases, etc.

8. What is the speed of sperm when it leaves the end of a man's penis during ejaculation?

c. 28 mph

See below.

9. How many sperm are contained in an average ejaculation?

d. 100 million

The purpose of semen is purely for reproduction – as a vehicle to carry the sperm into the female reproductive tract – and for this large numbers are needed to make the journey (as the great majority don't even get close) and a certain speed is needed to propel it into the vagina and towards the egg.

10. How many sperm are needed to fertilize a woman's egg so that she gets pregnant?

a. 1

And there is a 30 per cent likelihood that this will happen, meaning sexually active boys who do not use contraception have a 90 per cent chance of making someone pregnant within one year.

11. What is the legal age of consent for sexual intercourse in the UK?

b. 16

NB It is 17 in Northern Ireland (see Chapter 4).

12. What is the legal age of consent for gay sex in the UK?

a. 16

NB It is 17 in Northern Ireland (see Chapter 4).

13. What is the legal age of consent for lesbian sex in the UK?

a. 16

NB It is 17 in Northern Ireland (see Chapter 4).

14. On average, how many times do single males masturbate?

a. Two or three times a week

See Chapter 5.

15. On average, how many times do single females masturbate?

a. Two or three times a month

See Chapter 5.

16. In the UK, how many girls under the age of 16 have had sex?

b. 1 in 5

17. What is the risk of a young woman getting pregnant if she has unprotected sexual intercourse 14 days before her next period?

b. 30 per cent

18. Can you get pregnant during your period?

a. Yes

Simply because sperm can survive for 5–7 days, which means if you ovulate early you'll get pregnant.

19. Can you get pregnant if the man doesn't have an orgasm?
    a. Yes
    Although ejaculation of semen accompanies orgasm in men, erection and orgasm are controlled by separate mechanisms, which means a man can still get you pregnant without having an orgasm.

20. Can a girl get pregnant before she starts her periods?
    a. Yes
    Simply because it's impossible to say when your period will begin and you may have ovulated or be about to start when you have sex.

21. Can a woman get pregnant if the man doesn't actually put his penis inside her?
    a. Yes
    See below and Chapter 5.

22. Can you get pregnant if the man withdraws before he ejaculates?
    a. Yes
    Sperm is present in pre-cum before ejaculation so it's still really easy for sperm to enter the vagina without ejaculation.

23. Which country has the highest teenage pregnancy rate in the world?
    d. The USA
    Teenage pregnancy rates in the United States are twice as high as in England and Wales or Canada, and nine times as high as in Holland or Japan.

24. How long can the average sperm hang around in the average vagina?

    d. More than 5 days

25. What do condoms help to protect against?

    e. All of the above

For more on condoms see Chapter 5.

26. How long after having sexual intercourse is the emergency contraceptive pill (morning after pill) effective?

    c. 72 hours

For more on emergency contraception see Chapter 5.

27. How many times a year can a woman have the emergency contraceptive pill?

    d. More than four times

For more on emergency contraception see Chapter 5.

28. Where can a woman get the emergency contraceptive pill?

    e. All of the above

For more on emergency contraception see Chapter 5.

29. The emergency contraceptive pill is most effective if taken within 24 hours, but how effective?

    c. 95 per cent

The efficiency rate decreases the longer you wait to take it.

30. How effective is the contraceptive pill if taken
as instructed?
d. Nearly 100 per cent
Non-effective use is down to human error. For more on
the pill and contraception see Chapter 5.

31. What does STI stand for?
Sexually transmitted infection
These used to be known as STDs – sexually transmitted
diseases – and VD – venereal diseases.

32. Name three STIs.
See Chapter 6 for a list of all STIs.

33. The best precaution against catching or passing on an
STI is to:
c. Use a condom
See Chapter 6 for more on STI prevention.

34. Which of the following are signs that you might have an
STI?
e. All of the above
Though bear in mind that plenty of STIs have no symptoms,
so unprotected sex always needs to be checked out.

35. Can you catch an STI from a lavatory seat?
b. No

36. Can you get an STI from oral sex?

a. Yes

See Herpes, Chapter 6.

37. Do you always know when you've got a sexually transmitted infection?

b. No

See Chapter 6.

38. How many 16–25-year-old women have chlamydia in the UK?

b. 1 in 10

Overall cases of chlamydia soared past the 100,000 mark in 2004 and more than 1,000 cases were found in girls 15 and under! See Chapter 6 for more on this.

39. If you've got chlamydia, what symptoms might you have?

e. All of the above

40. For women, what is the possible long-term effect of contracting chlamydia?

e. All of the above

See Chapter 6 for more on this.

41. What is the name of the virus that causes AIDS?

HIV – Human Immuno-deficiency Virus

42. If a man has one-off unprotected sexual intercourse with a woman who is HIV+, what are the chances of his catching the virus?

d. 1 in 1,000

See Chapter 6 for more on this.

43. What is the most common STI in the UK?

a. Chlamydia

See Chapter 6 for more on this.

44. Where can a woman go to get a referral for an abortion?

e. All of the above

See Resources for more information.

45. What is the legal limit for an abortion?

d. Up to 24 weeks

See Chapter 6 for more on this.

46. Can a woman get an abortion free on the NHS?

a. Yes

47. What is the single most common risk when having an abortion?

b. Risk of infection

See Chapter 6 for more on this.

YOUR QUESTIONS ANSWERED

Q It's all well and good people saying sex education should happen in the home, but the truth is I feel embarrassed by the thought. It was never spoken about between my parents and me, and I am really shy even speaking to my husband about it. This is why I feel very uncomfortable about the thought of sitting with my ten-year-old and telling her the facts of life. What if she turns questions on me and asks me something personal or says a term I don't understand? I want her to respect me, not think I am a stupid person who gets embarrassed over sex.

A Your daughter will respect you if you're 100 per cent honest and open with her. If you want a place to start, why not begin with the fact that you're embarrassed talking about sex because your own sex education was limited. This will help her to understand where you're coming from and stop you feeling you have to ooze confidence with every word. It will also give you the opportunity to ask her what she'd like to know from you, thereby giving her the message that this is a two-way talk. It doesn't matter if she turns a question on you or asks you something you don't know. Just be honest with her. In the meantime, read up on the sex and relationship information in Chapters 2 and 3 – it will give you some idea of where and how to start.

Q I have recently tried to be really open with my kids about sex, but they recoiled in horror when I asked them if they were interested in sex or had any sexual urges. My eleven-year-old daughter just put her fingers in her ears and my fourteen-year-old son rolled his eyes and walked away. I want them to feel they can be open with me on these things but instead they're not interested in talking to me. Help!

A It's not that your children don't want to talk about these issues – it's just that your full-on approach put them off. If this is the first time you've discussed sex with them, your questions were too direct and too personal. You need to start in a less dramatic fashion and talk about these subjects in a broader way that takes the focus off their own lives and helps them to think about these issues in general. Use everyday life as a way to spark discussion. Scenarios in soap operas are particularly good for this, as they give you an ideal place to talk about infidelity, sexual responsibility and relationships. Start again and start slower, and if your kids keep retreating sit down with them and suggest you all lay your cards on the table and say why you're finding it so difficult. Admit you came on too strong and ask them what they think a good place to start would be.

Q I am willing to talk to my daughters (eleven and thirteen), about sex but I don't want them to have sex and relationship education at school because it's too explicit and I have strong views about how children shouldn't have sex until they are older and married. All the information they get about where to get condoms, the pill and abortion makes me angry and I just want to know how to get the abstinence message across, because whenever I bring it up, they say I don't live in the real world and ignore me.

A If you want your girls to delay sex you have to say more than 'Just say no', because this tactic doesn't work. To get them to listen to you, start by listening to what they are saying. Their response that 'you don't live in the real world' means your advice isn't helpful because in their real world sex is happening around them and they need more than what you're giving them to deal with that. I'm not saying you should disregard what you believe in, but give them the chance to make the right decision for themselves by providing real information to work with. This is not just the sex basics such as contraception advice, but also help on what makes a good relationship, how to avoid peer pressure and why waiting until you're ready works.

Q I have two sons aged eight and thirteen years and a daughter aged ten, and I want to talk to them all about sex and love. The problem is, while my daughter is quite mature for her age, her brothers aren't and whenever we start talking about sex the conversation becomes very silly because the boys start making jokes and then teasing her. My husband suggests dividing them up – he takes the talk with the boys and I do the one with our daughter, but this makes me uncomfortable. I want them to feel at ease with each other about this, not divided. How should we talk to them?

As sex and relationship education is an ongoing process, the simple way to solve your problem is to divide your kids for some of the talks and unite them for others. For instance, your daughter may well prefer to talk about periods and puberty alone with you so that she can ask questions without being teased, but may prefer to hear what her brothers and dad have to say about relationships and love. Also, try not to make every conversation a proper 'talk'; for instance, feed off comments your kids make over dinner about their friendships and/or TV and use these to instigate a general and then specific conversation around relationships, love and sex, and make it something that happens regularly. This will take away the embarrassed silliness that's so easy to fall into and it will help your kids to relax when they speak to you.

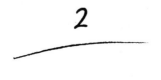

2

LET'S TALK SEX

CAN YOU TALK TO YOUR CHILDREN ABOUT SEX WITH A STRAIGHT face and/or answer potentially embarrassing questions without flinching in horror? If the answer's no, you're not alone. It's rare for many of us to be utterly frank like Kerry-Ann, who went as far as to buy her daughter Stephanie, fifteen, a vibrator for Christmas (though she readily admits that this was possibly a step too far and that her daughter was mortified). On the other hand she has talked openly about sex and relationships to Stephanie since she was young, with encouraging results. While I'm not suggesting in any way that you buy your kids sex toys, one of the huge benefits of talking openly about sex and relationships is ending up with confident kids who are able to delay sex and make decisions that are right for them.

Before I worked on these programmes the thought of talking to my own children about sex and relationships frightened the pants off me. I was worried about what to say, what not to say and what was the best way to answer an inquisitive five-year-old who wanted to know how she got into my tummy. Would I really be helping her if I told her the truth, or would I be confusing her even more if I made up a child-friendly story? Or worse still, if I simply changed the subject would I be storing up future trouble for myself?

Thankfully, through talking to a variety of teenagers and their parents, I now realize that the answer's simple – kids are looking for honest explanations to their questions, and talks at home that are casual and easy, rather than lesson-like and dull. Of course, this is easier said than done, which is why this chapter's all about how to talk to children as young as four and teenagers as old as fifteen about sex, love and all the rest. So even if your own sex and relationship education was a bit patchy, or if your children already seem to know more than you, there are some brilliant tried and tested ways to deal with those tricky questions.

Biological basics aside, good sex and relationship education, say the experts, is about instilling confidence, passing on good negotiating skills and showing your kids how to be open when it comes to sex. This means that before you start passing on words of wisdom, you need to know where you stand on all of the above. For most of us this means figuring out what it is you want to say about sex and love, how you're going to deliver it and what the latest and best sex advice is.

Of course, no sane teenager wants to hear from your mouth that you are having sex, never mind enjoying it, which is how most of them will translate any sex information that passes from your lips. This is just one reason why it pays to start early with your children. Talk about the weather and school for fourteen years and then suddenly throw them sex info, say something outrageously shocking, or put a condom on the table at dinnertime and your kids will make for the hills – and the subject will be silenced for ever within your house.

Thankfully there are some genius ways to entice even the most mortified teenager and parent out of their respective corners, such as starting off with the words, 'OK, this is embarrassing, but let's get over that bit and have a chat,' or encouraging your kids to do the talking first by discussing what you watch together on TV, or what they're reading. If you're wondering why you should even bother – considering that their school, their friends and even the odd sex and relationships book thrown their way could do the job for you – it's worth knowing that parents who can talk about sex and relationships at home tend to have children who will not only delay sex but will have a healthier attitude towards sex all round.

As for the argument that we should keep our children 'innocent' for as long as possible, you only have to switch on the TV to see that there is a staggering array of sexual imagery thrown at them every day, which means even if you're rigorous about keeping the conversation sex-free at home, your kids will already have started making assumptions about sex and love. This means they need your input, because it's easy to be confused by information that's inaccurate, inappropriate or simply puzzling.

It's also worth knowing that, despite their caginess, your teenagers do want to hear it from you. According to research from the Department of Health, young people say they do want to learn about sex and relationships from their parents and want more than just the biological facts. They want to talk about feelings and morals and want you to answer their questions, not just fob them off. Further research from the Sex Education Forum also shows that 'Children whose families are confident talking about sex and relationships find it easier to resist peer pressure and express their beliefs and opinions, and are able to understand the negative messages about sex and relationships.'

Lastly, and more importantly, information is power, and the clearer and more concise the information your teenagers have about sex and relationships from you, the better the decisions they can make about their own lives based on fact and reasoning rather than peer pressure and myth. And if none of the above stirs you into action, remember that sooner or later, whether your kids are fifteen or twenty-one or even older, they are going to fall in love and have sex one day – so help them to face it with the right confidence.

'My mum used to try to talk to me but I got embarrassed and then my dad tried but then I got really embarrassed because it was my dad. I can talk to my mum but I still don't feel right talking to her about sex.'

DIONNE, 16

THREE STEPS TO GET FROM EMBARRASSMENT TO TALKING

Step One: How to override your own embarrassment

As a parent, I totally understand that it's tempting to think of sex and relationship education as a way to frighten your children into keeping their pants on for life. None of us wants to think of some grubby little teen getting their hands on one of our little darlings. However, as the aim is to give your child a healthy attitude to sex and love, you have to override this dread. To start with, think about your own sex education:

- Was your information collected in the school playground, around the dinner table or through hidden fumbles behind the bike sheds?
- What do you wish your parents had said (or hadn't said) to you about sex?
- What do you know now that you wish you'd known at thirteen years old, eight years old and younger?
- How could your sex education have made you more confident about your body and your relationships?

In knowing what you missed out on and its repercussions in your life (by the way, how was your first experience of sex?), you can find a place to begin a conversation with your own children. And remember: this conversation, though embarrassing, doesn't have to be dry, stern or bland – especially if that's not the usual way you speak to your kids. Be yourself, or else they will know something is up and back off from you. Sex is never an easy subject to discuss, but the more you make yourself talk about it, the more you read about it, the less embarrassing and awkward it becomes.

This is important to remember, because for sex and relationship education to work it can't be a one-off session during which you throw everything you know into the pot, add a few words of warning and then consider it done. The best education is an ongoing one that involves answering questions, bringing up points and educating yourself at the same time as your children.

If you can get your kids to realize that your talks are a two-way thing, which needn't be all formal and serious, they'll be much more likely to come to you with their own questions and opinions. One good way to do this and to get over your embarrassment is first simply to get used to talking about sex with friends and partners. This is an ideal way to desensitize yourself, as well as to get used to using certain sexual terms and discussing sexual opinions and judgements. The more you talk about sex (and the less you do that nudge, nudge, wink, wink thing), the more confident you'll feel about explaining sexual topics at home. In turn, your kids will hear the confidence in your voice, which will make them feel safe about discussing more topics with you.

Help yourself by:

- Discussing sex and relationship education worries with other parents.
- Talking about sexual issues and morals with friends to help you consider your own judgements.
- Educating yourself about sex through sex-education books and leaflets (see Resources for more information on this).
- Talking with your partner about how to tackle the more sensitive areas with your kids.
- Discussing what went wrong or right with your own sex education.
- Considering your own feelings and expectations about sex and relationships.

'I never really spoke to my dad about sex. He did try to tell me that I should act a certain way and that I shouldn't sleep around but I know that even though that's how he wants me to be that's not necessarily how he was when he was young.'

RORY, 18

'With my parents sex was designed for one thing only. Nowadays it's a leisure thing, like going to the pub.'

STEVEN, 18

Step Two: How to make an early start

Sex and relationship education that works basically starts early – that's before puberty, and before your kids have decided they are 100 per cent sure that they know everything and don't need anything more from you (which happens earlier than you may think). If you stay alert, even very young children will tell you when they're ready to know something, and they will learn from your response whether sex is something they can discuss with you or something they need to hide from you. For instance, many young children are naturally inquisitive and will bombard you with questions about 'Why has Dad got a willy while I don't?' 'What are those things on your chest?' Or they will naturally play with their sexual organs to soothe themselves to sleep, or just for fun (which can be shocking to see but is natural).

How you react does tend to set the pattern for sex education in your house. Tell them off for asking an embarrassing question, act shocked or simply feed them an untrue story such as 'The stork brings a baby' or 'You'll go blind if you touch yourself', and you're asking for trouble later on. Passing on myths not only makes your children distrust you when they discover the truth but also makes them feel that sex is something you can't handle discussing. Real information at an early age and in appropriate language will not only show them that you can be trusted to give the right information but will also give them an acceptance of their own body and help provide a good foundation on which you can add more and more knowledge as time goes on.

Of course, not all children are so questioning and inquisitive about sex. Some will not ask you a single question, whether from lack of interest or from fear, which is why it also pays to be proactive about sex and relationship education. Don't think your child is too young just because they don't seem interested or assume they know already because they seem so smart and self-aware. Remember, we don't wait for kids to ask questions over other things we think are important, such as crossing the road, we simply bring it up and talk it over with them to help them make decisions that will protect them. This same attitude needs to be applied to sex and relationship education.

'If I had a son I'd say enjoy yourself, but if I had a daughter I'd keep her under lock and key. I wouldn't want her to get used. It's different with boys and girls.'

RORY, 18

'I never went up to my mum and asked her about sex and puberty – it was more her telling me, saying you'll be on your period soon. But when I got older I asked her because I was comfortable talking about it with her and felt close enough too.'

KERRY, 16

'I feel too embarrassed to talk to my mum. I ask my sister because at school we get no information apart from stuff about babies.'

LEANNE, 14, Kerry's sister

Step Three: How to talk so they listen

Information aside, good sex and relationship education is all in the delivery. How you talk about sex is as important as what you talk about, because much of what your children will pick up about what can and can't be said will come from your tone and actions.

Think about your language and tone

Your kids call sex 'fucking' or 'shagging' – should you? Well, there's nothing more likely to have them recoiling in horror than you trying to speak to them in their language. Not only will they spot in an instant that you're trying to 'bond', but it will make them cringe, taking the focus off your message and stopping them from hearing what you're saying. To get your point across speak normally, otherwise they'll feel you're being insincere. However, it is worth trying to update your phrases, especially if you haven't discussed sex since you were in the school playground yourself. For instance, use the word sex rather than making love, breast rather than boobs, and condom rather than rubber/Johnny. Read up on how sex and relationships are spoken about by looking at the websites and books aimed at children of various ages (see Resources). Above all, aim to be genuine! Your kids know you better than anyone and they will hear any lies, confusion or embarrassment in your voice. They'll trust you more if you're honest with them about feeling embarrassed and awkward at times.

Try to be non-judgemental

Obviously this is hard, as you're not an objective observer but an emotionally attached parent whose first reaction is to protect your child. However, your kids will never trust you if you start telling them that their views are wrong or if you come over all judgemental and parental about sex. Consider Kerry-Ann's reaction when her fifteen-year-old daughter's boyfriend, Danny, came to her asking if they could get engaged. 'Originally I felt myself go to do that mother thing of you're too young, don't be so bloody stupid, but saying you're too young to be in love doesn't make it any less intense for them. They are feeling love. They might not be feeling adult, fully grown love, but they are feeling love. So many people don't respect their children enough to let them have their own opinions but right now, she loves him.'

Of course, personal judgements are hard to overturn, especially if your views are guided by cultural or religious values. To get round this, on the one hand try to be honest with your children about your values, opinions and expectations about sex, because they'll pick up on them anyway, but on the other be wary of getting into an 'I'm right, you're wrong' type of discussion. Turn your talks into a battle of wills and the subject will just become a fight for power, rather than a discussion about sex and sexual responsibility.

Also beware of telling young people not to have sex; it rarely works and is often a total waste of breath. Finally, as much as you might hate it, try to accept that your views may not end up being your kids' views, but if you can teach them to be smart about their sexual choices you'll have done your job well.

Keep an open mind

Sexual attitudes change all the time. It doesn't mean you have to change your attitude to stay in fashion but rather that you need to be open to what your kids are saying to you. If you overreact, condemn everything or try to make them accept that you're right, they'll be less likely to talk to you when they are feeling pressured, unsure or concerned about issues relating to sex. Help yourself by keeping up to date with what's going on in the news and on TV, and before you discuss anything think about how you're going to respond to information you don't agree with and to revelations from your children that you don't want to hear.

Think about:

- What you'll do if they disagree with you.
- How you're going to cope if they have radically different views to you over subjects such as homosexuality and underage sex.

At the same time, however, don't be afraid to say what you think. For instance, your teenager may think that having sex at fourteen is fine because all her friends are doing it, but if this dismays you, say so – but also explain why. Likewise, if your son or daughter has started using lots of sexual swear words, don't be afraid to stop them, again telling them why these words are inappropriate and explaining why they offend.

Be trustworthy with their information

Also known as 'Don't share your kid's personal questions with friends and family'. There's nothing more likely to make your teenagers turn away from you than making a joke out of how they feel. As mum Kerry-Ann says, 'When you're a teenager you feel things so strongly and it's so intense, and for people to turn around and say you're stupid and you're not old enough to feel that, it's soul destroying. It rips the arse out of your good feelings.'

To respect their privacy avoid:

- Laughing at them because you think their question sounds ridiculous.
- Overreacting because you're worried by the nature of their questions.
- Putting them down for having different opinions to yours.
- Belittling their feelings – for instance, telling them they're not in love when they say they are.
- Telling other family members and friends what they have said as a joke.

Practise active listening

If your kids constantly moan, 'You don't listen to me' – maybe you don't. In the adult world we're all so quick to say our bit and get our views out that we often forget how to listen, especially when tired, ratty and trying to make the dinner. If you want your teenagers to hear you, hear them. Active listening is a technique whereby you let someone speak without interrupting (no matter how badly you want to) and then paraphrase his or her words back them. It allows you to:

- Ensure you heard their side correctly.
- Let them know you've heard them.

It lets them know you are listening and gives you the space to reply.

Try not to control their decisions

If you're someone who is used to making decisions and taking control of situations, it can be hard just to sit back and let your children become independent thinkers – i.e. make their own decisions. And it's particularly hard if you feel the choices they are making aren't the right ones. As tempting as it is to step in and take control, don't do it (unless the situation is potentially dangerous). Your kids won't thank you for it and, instead of seeing it as support, they'll read it as control and push the other way. In order to build confidence, your children need to make mistakes and learn from them, so make sure you allow them to:

- Make decisions that you know aren't going to work out with their relationships and friendships.

- Work their way through why something didn't work out.
- Evaluate situations by themselves without you telling them what to think and do.

Be honest about the good side of sex

Come on, let's be honest, your teenagers aren't going to believe you if you try to tell them sex is bad and go on about teen pregnancy, sexual infections and the pain and misery of sex. Everyone knows there is an enjoyable and tantalizing aspect to sex and discussing this alongside the scarier elements will give them a healthy attitude, as well as help them to formulate expectations that are more realistic.

- Emphasize the positive by talking about sex and relationships as being enjoyable and fun.
- Use relationships that are in the public eye or that your kids have witnessed as examples of how relationships can work well.

WHAT TO TALK ABOUT

All children are made differently, so what works for one kid doesn't work for another and what one kid needs, another knows, which means you need to take a pick-and-mix attitude to your sex and relationship education based on each individual child. Rather than trying to squeeze everything in and driving yourself bonkers in the process, the answer is to cover what you feel is essential and what your kids ask you about. The following is a selection of issues that are worth discussing. Choose the ones that you feel are most needed for your child.

Sexual responsibility

In terms of self-esteem and confidence, sexual responsibility is one of the most important areas to discuss, especially in terms of the consequences that come from not looking after your health. Talking to your kids about looking after their bodies is also a good way to talk about self-worth.

Areas to talk about:

- **Falling in love.** Try using anecdotal stories, storylines from the TV shows that you watch, and with younger children stories from their own books, to spark discussion (for more on this see Chapter 5).
- **Sexual health risks of multiple partners.** Check out Chapter 6 for information on STIs and their repercussions.
- **Contraception.** Discuss the different methods, the concept of Double Dutch (Chapter 5) and how to deal with partners who won't use contraception. This is also a good point to talk about confidentiality and other people that they can approach for confidential help and advice.
- **How to protect yourself emotionally.** Discuss peer pressure, standing up to friends, how it feels when someone lets you down and where to turn for help and support (Chapter 5).
- **Love and sexual expectations.** What opinions do your kids hold about falling in love? Do they believe in love at first sight and that love conquers all? Do they think that fireworks go off when you have sex? Or even that sex equals love? (For more on this see Chapter 5.)

Feeling normal

Everyone (even the most sorted adult) worries sometimes that somehow they are not normal. This, however, is emphasized during puberty thanks to lopsided boobs, wet dreams, unwanted erections or strange fantasies – meaning your kids are going to be worried about their changing bits. The problem is, if they are unable to discuss these worries with someone they trust, they can go on into adulthood fearing they are somehow impaired and this will affect their relationship choices. Openness about bodies in general and passing on accurate information about growth, hormones and sex will help to lessen their angst and increase their body confidence.

Areas to talk about:

- **Puberty and what to expect** (see Chapter 3).
- **Body image – and media images.** Look at the magazines, videos and films your kids are watching and reading. Listen to who their heroes are and why. Then use this as a way to discuss body images and how they feel about themselves.
- **Feelings and sexual urges.** Even very young children get crushes on favourite relatives, pop stars or even teachers and this is an ideal way to talk to them about love and feelings. Sexual urges are harder, simply because your older kids may not want to admit that they have them (or realize what they are), so it pays to prepare them by talking about the difference between love and lust and the concept of sexual attraction.

- **What's normal and what's not.** This is an essential area to focus on with your teenagers, especially if you don't want them to feel frightened and alone when their body starts changing. A practical and informative approach is best if both of you are embarrassed.
- **Emotional highs and lows of puberty.** Likewise prepare them (and yourself) for the emotional rollercoaster of feelings and moods they may go through. A good way to do this is to use your own moods and hormonal sways as a way into discussing things like frustration, anger and sadness.

Self-esteem and body image

Several studies, including one by the Commonwealth Fund in America of 7,000 kids, have documented that, when they enter puberty, young girls in particular experience a crisis in confidence that renders them vulnerable to risky health behaviours that they may not have the strength or will to resist. Partly fuelled by the fact they are teenagers, most children are fairly likely to have some form of low self-esteem as result of the comparisons kids naturally make between what they see on TV and in magazines, and amongst their friends, and what they see reflected back in the mirror. According to the above study, only 39 per cent of girls said they were highly self-confident and some older girls had less self-esteem than the younger ones. Girls were also more likely to be critical of themselves, with 25 per cent of girls and 14 per cent of boys reporting that they did not like, or even hated, themselves.

To help instil good self-esteem you need to help your kids to hone their individual talents and skills and set goals for the future that make them realize their self-worth.

Areas to talk about:

- **How to have the confidence to be yourself.** This is about belief in yourself – so you need to get your children to focus on their gut feelings and how to stand up for what they believe is right, whether that's to do with how their friends treat them or with beliefs they have about society in general.
- **How to like yourself.** Help your kids to focus on their talents and strengths rather than on all the things they are going to start feeling they don't have. Reinforce these beliefs by telling them what you feel they are great at, whether it's academic, social or practical skills.
- **How you treat yourself.** This is about not being too hard on yourself and silencing the critic within. Girls in particular will turn in on themselves if their self-esteem is low, so again you need to get them to focus on speaking to themselves in a positive voice and giving themselves a break when things go wrong. Steer them away from the concept of perfection.

Negotiation and communication skills in relationships

One way to give your children more confidence is to encourage them to ask questions and think about what they believe. As annoying as all the 'Why?' questions are, allowing yourself to be a source of information and discussion will help you to determine their level of knowledge and understanding and allow them to see that they can ask questions and consider the answers without feeling belittled. This in turn can help them to weigh up the pros and cons of a situation and help them make informed choices in their relationships without feeling under peer pressure.

Areas to talk about:

- **How to say no to friends.** Discuss with them how you have learnt to do this and what being a good friend means.
- **Peer pressure in general.** What it is and how it may affect them (or is affecting them already).
- **Doing things to fit in.** This is about their need to belong and be one of the crowd, so focus on individuality alongside compromise, and on the highs and lows of friendships.

The opposite sex

If your kids have siblings of the opposite sex and go to a mixed school, it's likely they already know how to talk to the opposite sex and how to fight with them. If not, their views of the opposite sex may be somewhat wonky and in need of some discussion. Shattering myths about what men and women want and what men and women are like, as well as discussing the biological facts of the opposite sex, can help your children develop a healthy attitude towards love and sex and towards the opposite sex, as well as helping them to see that they have equal status.

You may think it's too early (or just too political) to discuss gender beliefs, but from an early age kids decide what girls do and what boys do through their play, the toys they use and even through what they read and watch, so you need to determine what it is your children believe. Let them decide for themselves without your input and you run the risk of them taking their views into adulthood. Do they, for instance, think men should have jobs and women stay at home (old-fashioned, but you'd be amazed at how many little girls think this)? Have they picked up messages from your relationship about who gets to be in control, or have they picked up from the stories they've been reading how men and women behave when they are in love?

Areas to talk about:

- **Double standards.** Do your kids believe that men and women should be treated differently? Do they believe men and women want different things from relation-ships? Do they hold different sets of values for men and women? These are good questions that will not only set them thinking but also build a base for you to discuss double standards in sex and relationships later on.
- **The physical differences between sexes** (see Chapter 3).
- **What they believe the differences are between the sexes.** What beliefs do they hold about what women can do compared to men and vice-versa? From a very young age children will already hold quite strong views on this, so watch how your toddlers play, or listen out for the comments your pre-teen makes about boys or girls.

How to deal with unwanted sexual attention and information

As difficult as it is for you, it's essential to talk with your kids about unwanted sexual attention. Hopefully it will never happen to your child but, if it does, giving them the tools to deal with it will not only help them to seek help immediately but also will not leave them at the mercy of a manipulative older or stronger person. Stress from an early age that their bodies are their own and no-one has the right to touch them, say things or ask them to do things that make them feel uncomfortable, or make them look at things (both in person or via email) if they don't want to. Reinforce this message as they get older, discussing privacy, sexual language and how to listen to their gut feelings.

Areas to talk about:

- How to listen to what feels right and what feels wrong. This is about getting them to identify their gut feelings and teaching them how to go with these instincts even if it means disagreeing with someone older, an adult, a family member, or with a group of friends. Describe this feeling as their inner alarm warning them that things aren't right.
- How to say no to anyone they know. Many boys and girls are afraid to disagree with or to say no to an adult, so you need to give them the confidence to see that in some situations it's their right to stand up for themselves. Teach them specific tactics on how to be assertive, how to shout for help, where to go for help and who to tell when they're afraid.

AGE-SPECIFIC DISCUSSIONS

As you already know, all children are made differently. There are some who just won't stop asking questions and others who just don't seem aware of the world, which is why the following approach can be really helpful in reaching both younger children and shy children. This tactic not only helps your kids open up over the questions they feel awkward about expressing, but also helps start an ongoing conversation between the two of you.

Start by leaving a blank notebook with a pen somewhere where your child has access to it, and let them know that if there's any question or query (not just about sex and relationships) that they really want to ask you but are too afraid/embarrassed to ask, they should note it down in the book, saying whether they want a reply in person or in the book. Agree with them in advance that if they don't want to discuss it outside the book, you won't bring it up (and be sure to keep to this, as it shows they can trust you). In replying, always ask questions back so you can see how much they have understood and use their questions as a way to spark a new discussion.

This is an ideal way to help your child form the habit of turning to you about anything that's bothering them and it will help you to build confidence and openness in them.

Here are some ideas of what needs to be discussed at relevant ages. Again, choose what's right for your son or daughter.

Curious toddlers

From about eighteen months onwards, most children become curious about their own bodies and the bodies of others. They'll start pointing out things in the bathroom, poking around in general or examining their bits in greater detail. This makes it a good time to begin telling your child the proper names for sex organs. While it's tempting to use funny, child-friendly names – especially if you feel uncomfortable about saying 'penis' and 'vagina' – bear in mind that what you say now is what your kids will use later.

Likewise, it's about this time that you may spot your child touching his or her sex organs, or examining a friend. This can be shocking to see (ask any other parent) but it's 100 per cent normal, so, tempting as it is to shout 'Stop!', be wary of making them feel they are doing something bad. Instead use this as a way to talk about privacy. Emphasize that their bodies are private and that certain things need to done away from other people.

Also with very young children, try to answer their questions honestly but in an age-appropriate way. For instance, if your daughter asks why she doesn't have a penis, point out that only men and boys do. If your son asks where babies come from, don't go into scientific detail, but tell him babies grow in mummies' tummies. As they get older you can fill in the missing blanks and add more information that they can (a) understand and (b) get interested in.

Inquisitive tweenies

Between the ages of three and five your children's curiosity about the world, their bodies, your body and other people's bodies will reach a peak. Most kids around this time want to know why their bodies do some things or why their bodies look different to yours. Spark discussion by following what they are interested in. Point out babies and pregnant women, using this as a way to talk to them more about where babies come from. Bear in mind, though, that by this age children may already be confused about babies and bodies and men and women, so start by asking what your child knows about a particular topic before you dive in and start explaining it.

Remember, you don't have to explain anything in intricate detail – just start passing on accurate information that gives a clear picture. If you have a tweenie you'll know how aware of the world they are and how they question everything they view. You'll probably be freaked out by some of their questions, but be aware that they are just looking for an answer from you that sounds logical, not an in-depth discussion (their attention spans couldn't handle that anyway). A simple, honest answer at this age is enough for most children.

Be aware too that sometimes very young children ask a question because they are trying to understand something they have heard or seen on TV. So if the question seems shocking to you, it's not that their knowledge base is higher than you anticipated but rather that they are trying to figure something out, which is why it's important to ask, 'Where did you see/ hear that?'

For example, your four-year-old may ask you:

Question: How did I get in your tummy?
Answer: Daddy put a seed in there and you grew into a baby.

Question: Why haven't I got a thingy like Dad/my brother?
Answer: Because you're a girl and you have a vagina, which doesn't stick out, and boys have a penis that does stick out.

Question: What's sex?
Answer: It's the way two grown-up people show love to each other.

Question: Do you and daddy have sex?
Answer: Yes, because we're adults and we like and love each other.

Question: Why are they kissing with tongues?
Answer: It's a way some adults who love each other kiss.

Pre-teen angst

Primary-school children need age-appropriate information more than ever, especially as puberty is starting earlier. Under new guidelines set by the Qualification and Curriculum Authority (QCA), issued in November 2005, by Key Stage 1 (age seven) children should be able to do the following:

- Recognize the effect of their behaviour on other people.
- Identify and respect differences and similarities between people.
- Recognize and name the main body parts.
- Know that humans can produce children.

By Key Stage 2 (age eleven) they should:

- Be aware of the main human life cycles.
- Know about the emotional and bodily changes at puberty and how to deal with these in a positive way.
- Know how to develop a healthy lifestyle.
- Identify factors that affect emotional health and well-being.

The above are supposed to be covered within Personal, Social and Health Education but, as schools are not obliged to teach the non-science aspects at primary level, your kids may only be learning about the biological facts of sex. This is just one reason to have conversations that start broadening their scope and include topics such as puberty, feelings and relationships.

Pre-puberty you will notice some sexual development in your child in terms of behaviour. You may find, for instance, that they suddenly become shy about being naked in front of you or insist on more privacy, both in the bathroom and in their bedroom. If you're a parent who likes to wander around in the buff, it pays to respect your children's wishes in terms of their own feelings about modesty and not force them to adhere to yours.

You may also spot them getting crushes on famous people or talking to their friends about love, sex and kissing, or even reading magazines with scantily clad celebrities in. Again, tempting as it is to laugh or lay down the law, use these things as a springboard for discussion.

What your pre-teens want to know

More than anything, primary-school children between the ages of eight and eleven worry about whether they are 'normal' – as seen by the hundreds of letters sent to teen-magazine advice columns every month. So don't assume your child isn't aware of puberty just because they haven't yet experienced any body changes. Also be aware that, for most primary-school kids, puberty is a race they can't win. On the one hand they don't want to be left behind and be the last to grow/get their period/have a boyfriend or girlfriend, and yet they also don't want to be the first. This is why penis size and breast size figure heavily in most of these early worries. Children need reassuring that (a) they will develop and (b) their development is normal. You also need to emphasize:

- Bodies come in all shapes and sizes. Use TV and magazines to emphasize this and as a way to discuss feelings they may have about their own bodies.
- The importance of a good body image in terms of how feeling good or bad about your body will affect your self-esteem and self-worth. Get them to think about good days and bad days and how a change in emotion can make them feel differently about themselves.
- Good nutrition to help your body work properly and to feel positive about your body. Also get them thinking about all the good things their body can do and how what they eat and how they exercise affects it.
- Peer pressure over how to dress, act and behave. A good way to find out how they feel about this is to talk to them about what's going on with their friends and how they

feel about certain friends and how their friends make them feel.

- Mixed emotions about growing up and growing older, and the positive aspects of becoming a teenager.

Good ways to discuss the points above are to use magazine articles, and even soap-opera plots and films, as a way into a discussion. Also try to get your child to focus on a role model whom they can admire for a variety of reasons aside from their status and looks, as this will get them to focus on inner talents as well as exterior ones.

Answering embarrassing questions

Think your child is still 'innocent' when it comes to knowing about sex? Well don't be surprised if your pre-teen comes home and asks you about blow jobs or the 69 position or even orgasms. Primary-school-aged kids are exposed to much more than we think these days, which means you need to be ready to explain to your eight-year-old things that you may not feel they're ready to know simply because they are asking about it. If, for instance, the blow job question comes up:

- Start by asking where they heard this term and what do they think it means. This will help you to see where their sexual knowledge is at.
- If your child has a certain amount of knowledge, try explaining that people experience sexual pleasure in a variety of ways, including kissing and hugging, and touching each other's genitals, emphasizing the relationship aspect of sex.

- If your pre-teen has a clearer picture of sex, then you could emphasize that a blow job is a different way for two people to experience sexual pleasure, which involves kissing and licking the genitals.
- Unless your child has a very clear idea of the intricacies of sex, avoid a technical and mechanical description until they are older and capable of understanding oral sex in more depth.
- After you have explained the above, ask them to reflect back what you have said, as this is a good way to assess what they have learnt and understood.

Self-esteem and your pre-teen

We're all human and that means we all hate to do things that are uncomfortable and hard, which is why most kids struggle when the going gets tough near puberty. What you have to remember is that stepping outside the comfort zone – which is essentially what happens during puberty – is hard and that's the reason why pre-teens need so much emotional support. The downside of puberty is the constant negative comparisons we all learn to make, whereby we convince ourselves that we are uglier/stupider/fatter/thinner and more abnormal than everyone else.

One way to help your children boost their self-esteem as part of their sex education is to get them to value their body and what it can do as well as to see their strengths and skills. To get them motivated, encourage them to:

- **Say positive things to themselves.** Point out that saying horrible things about your own body and abilities not only stops you from doing something positive but also encourages you to do something negative to comfort yourself.

- **Inspire them.** Ask them whom they admire and what they can learn from that person. Is it a footballer's amazing achievements, a pop star's transformation, a favourite teacher's or friend's personal achievement? If they feel very uninspired, take the time to help find a role model with them by reading magazine or newspaper interviews with famous people, searching the biography section of the library and/or surfing the net to find out more about anyone's story they can relate to. The inspiration doesn't have to be a famous person, as role models work even better if it's someone they know, or someone they can actually go and talk to.

- **Help them set realistic goals.** Get your kids to be realistic about what they are aiming for. Help them choose goals that are both short term and long term. Short-term goals are essential because if they don't see some results for their hard work in a few weeks then they'll lose motivation. Short-term goals can be anything from joining in and learning a new sport, and/or saying nice things to themselves all week, or counting to ten before losing their temper. A long-term goal may be something like getting fit, getting a role in the school play, or even changing the way they feel about themselves.

- **Get them to move out of 'If only...' land.** Many children with low self-esteem live in 'If only...' land. For example, 'If only I were prettier/smarter/thinner ... I would be happier.' These are just diversions that allow your kids to avoid dealing with their problems face on. Get them to see that if they hate something about themselves, such as doing badly at school or their body weight, then they should focus on the solution not the problem.

Teenagers – the tunnel years

If you've got a teenager you're probably already experiencing what I call the tunnel years – a time when your previously sweet angelic child goes into a tunnel and becomes shut off to new ideas issuing from you, making your job about a hundred times harder. The skills teenagers need at this stage of their sex and relationship education are different to the skills younger children need, and are linked both to life skills and to thinking processes such as how to relate to others, manners and morals. By this point, under Key Stage 3 (age fourteen) and Key Stage 4 (age sixteen) of the National Curriculum, they should know all the emotional and physical changes that take place during puberty. Besides this they may need help with decision-making, communication, listening, negotiating and asserting themselves (though you may well disagree with the last point), so again pick and mix from the following.

Of course, the main problem with talking to older kids is that most don't want to admit they don't know things. So if your older children shrug off your attempts to talk about sex or say they know all about it, then you need to start discussions by feeding off random questions and statements they make (or obviously don't make) about sex, relationships and the way people treat each other. These discussions should help you see what they know and what they don't know about:

- What makes a good relationship besides fancying each other.
- Sexually transmitted infections – do they know how they are passed, what the symptoms are (if any) and what to do if they suspect they have one (see Chapter 6 for more details).
- Responsible sexual behaviour – including the needs and feelings of their partner.
- Contraception and safe sex (see Chapter 5 for more on this).

Be aware, however, that in their quest to become more independent, your kids are going to attempt to distance themselves from you in any way that they can. This means you must expect a certain amount of defiance, discontent and restlessness alongside high emotions – a tantalizing mix for you, so if you want to talk to them effectively try the following:

- **Treat your teenager as an adult.** Aim for mutual respect, and support. This is not always easy or practical, but as long as you stay true to your beliefs about manners, rudeness and respect, eventually your child will understand the boundaries you're setting and hopefully will take these lessons into their own relationships.

   At the same time, use praise and trust to help build their self-esteem and recognize your teens' feelings by listening when they talk about their relationships.
- **Remember that listening doesn't mean you have to solve your son's or daughter's problems or even that they want you to solve them.** It also doesn't mean that you

have to agree with their solutions, nor that you should hold back if you feel they are doing something wrong.

- **Avoid harsh criticism.** Negative relationships grow when you criticize a teenager too much. How they dress, talk and act is a bid for independence (as well as a bid for a reaction), so try to avoid attacking your teenager's lifestyle choices, especially when it comes to partners and friends. This doesn't mean withholding your views but allowing them to start making their own decisions and mistakes (within reason, obviously) so that they can start learning about the highs and lows of relationships.

- **Don't be their best friend.** Teenagers are looking for a parent to set boundaries, not a parent who acts like their best friend. This means you have the responsibility for making rules regarding your house and for setting consequences. This establishes clear rules about acceptable behaviour that they can use in other areas of life and in other relationships.

- **Give them space.** Generally when your teenager is in a bad mood or upset, they won't want to talk about it with you and certainly won't want you trying to pry into their angst. In general, it is best to give them space and privacy until they are ready to come to you – though obviously within reason in terms of both behaviour within the home and time spent distancing themselves.

Issues to discuss with your teenager

At this stage of their sex and relationship education, focus your attention on subject areas that deal with dilemmas, morals and responsibility, so that you can get them to think about their beliefs and about what they would do in a tricky situation before they actually get into one.

Sexuality – homosexuality, bisexuality or heterosexuality?

While some people know from a young age that they are gay, others think they know and then discover differently as they get older. But it's during puberty that people can often feel attracted to a member of the same sex, feel they are gay or display prejudice towards people with a different sexuality to their own. These are just a few reasons why it pays to discuss sexuality in some depth. Of course, your own feelings may well come to the fore here, which is why it's important to try to keep an open mind if your beliefs are strong and one-sided.

If your child is telling you they might be gay, don't dismiss it as a 'phase', get angry or tell them they're not. They are trying to tell you they are worried, afraid and feel different, meaning that they are looking for reassurance and help from you, not judgements. Try to emphasize that they should take time in deciding how they feel and ask if they would like to speak to someone independent (see Chapter 4; and also see Resources for the London Lesbian and Gay Switchboard). Likewise, don't be eager to attach a label to them or go out of your way to persuade them that they're wrong about their feelings.

Even if your child knows he or she is straight, then a discussion about sexuality is still essential, especially in terms of homophobia, prejudice and accepting other people's lifestyles and sexual decisions. Respecting differences and knowing when to practise tolerance is a good angle to take with relationships in general, especially with the emphasis on accepting people for who they are.

Ways to discuss this include:

- Discussing first impressions – by looking at times when you were both right and wrong.
- Keeping an open mind about sexuality and widening your circle of friends so that your judgements can be challenged! For instance, it may be easier to spend time with people who seem just like you (something we all do), but emphasize that you can miss out on a lot of interesting experiences by staying closed off.

Healthy and unhealthy relationships

Let's be honest: being a teenager is tough and lonely and this is why teens can find themselves falling into relationships that are unhealthy and unhappy but ultimately difficult to get out of, which is why you need to talk to your teenager about unhealthy relationships – not just in terms of sex, but also bullying, manipulation and aggression. Give them tools to boost their confidence and show them how to deal with difficult relationships so that you won't have to worry when they fall in love. Signs that they may be in a bad relationship include:

- New behaviours that are out of character.
- Withdrawal and mood swings.
- Comments that they feel inferior and worthless compared to a 'friend'/boyfriend/girlfriend.
- Signs of bullying – lack of money, lost possessions, and becoming unconfident in general.
- Self-destructive behaviour/self-harming.
- A change in eating habits.
- Bursts of unexplained anger.

To help them work out what to do, discuss what constitutes a good relationship and what constitutes a bad one (soap operas are an excellent basis for discussion here). Talk about learning how to say no to people; not feeling pressured into doing something you don't really want to do; and asserting yourself without aggression. Good ways to help a teenager with low confidence in these areas is to role-play scenarios (this doesn't have to be in the first person). Pose a dilemma, but be careful that you don't make it too close to the bone. Use scenarios that get your teen to think rationally and to offer advice as well as thinking about it from his or her own angle. For example:

Dilemma 1: X feels she can't say no to her friends because they won't want to be friends with her any more if she does. What do you think she should do? Why do you think she feels like this?

Dilemma 2: X is easily persuaded by his or her friends into doing things that feel risky – what are good ways to stand up to these friends without losing their friendships?

Dilemma 3: X is afraid to say she doesn't want to have sex because she thinks Y will dump her if she does. What should she do? What does this say about Y?

Dilemma 4: X gets aggressive when people tell him what to do. He hates authority and being bossed about – how can he be assertive without frightening people?

FINALLY, LET GO

We're all vulnerable when it comes to forming relationships and falling in love – and not just when it happens the first time. Who hasn't done something they regretted or felt the humiliation of rejection or the misery of being let down by someone you trusted? It's a hard thing to teach someone, and even harder to watch someone you love go through it. Part of the problem with sex and relationship education is that there comes a stage where you just need to let go and allow your teenager to move away from the theoretical towards the practical. You may not agree with what they do, but in order for your kids to understand fully all the information that you're giving them you need to let go and allow them to make their own decisions about dating, falling in love and sex. If you've supplied them with relationship skills and all the sex information and help they need, you can rest assured that they have a higher chance of making a responsible choice about what's right for them and what isn't.

THE OTHER SIDE OF THE COIN
Sex and Relationship Education and Your Parents

OK, taking the burden off your parents for a bit, here are a few pointers on how to talk about sex with your parents if you're a teenager. Before you think 'No way', or 'But they don't understand...', or 'They always get it wrong...', remember your parents weren't handed a manual when they got you, meaning they will stuff up now and again, say the wrong thing and irritate you in their quest to 'help', but it pays to give them a break, especially because they can be an excellent source of information.

Remember, if one day you want to be in a relationship in which you can talk about sex easily (plus have someone to go to with your worries and problems), it pays to learn how to make sex an open subject in your own home.

First and most important, if you want to talk about a specific sexual issue, avoid shock tactics. While it's amusing to see your parents wince and cringe, saying something just to get a reaction weakens your position and reinforces your parents' belief that you don't know what you're talking about. If you want them to take you seriously, show them that you can talk seriously about sex and the issues that bother you.

Second, you may be thinking 'Why bother?' Well, a good, open relationship with your parents can have a dual function when it comes to sex and relationship education. Not only are parents a good sounding board for your ideas and beliefs (even if you end up disagreeing), but they also have information at their fingertips, not to mention life experience that they can pass on. Plus – and this is a BIG plus – if you can talk about sex in an honest and open way at home, you're less likely to have hang-ups about sex, having sex and the opposite sex. Here's how to keep the lines of communication open.

Learn to talk to them

The best way you can communicate with your parents is to keep talking to them, no matter how mad or irritated you may be feeling. Remember, relationships aren't made better by two people distancing themselves from each other. Think about how much you talk to your best friends and how much you get out of it and how well they know you as a result of this. The same applies to parents. If you never say anything to them, how are they supposed to get things right about you?

Try to talk about ordinary everyday stuff with your parents as it's this that will build a connection with them that eventually will allow you to speak about things you find awkward and embarrassing. That doesn't mean you have to tell them everything or start having deep and meaningful conversations all the time. It means learning to see them as people who have something to offer you besides boring parental stuff. To get the ball rolling ask them questions for a change.

- Find out how they learnt about sex – this can be amusing from your own point of view and can help your parents to loosen up about sex in general.
- Ask them what embarrassing stuff happened to them

when they were growing up – again this opens an avenue for you to talk about your own worries.

- Try to discover what they were most worried about as teenagers.

Don't talk defensively

Also known as 'Don't assume that a question they ask you is loaded or a manipulative response unless you're 100 per cent sure that's what's being said.' For instance, when your parents ask you a question about where you are going or about sex, do you immediately assume they are being nosy? Do you read their interest in your life as them not trusting you? Is your response to shut down and turn away?

If so, it's worth knowing that your parents ask questions because they want to show they're interested in your life and they usually have no idea you find their questions so annoying. If you then shut down, they'll just assume the worst, such as that you have a problem or that you're hiding something, which in turn will lead to confrontations and more misunderstandings.

The way round this is to consider what's being said to you before you make a retort.

- If every question your parent asks you irritates you, then is it the nature of the questions, the way you are being asked or your general attitude to your parents that is to blame?
- If you dismiss everything they say as being wrong, is it because you don't trust their views or because you feel you know more than them?
- How do your parents respond to you when you are defensive?

- If you don't want to tell your parents how you feel about your life, have you considered why you feel this way?
- Do you know how your parents feel about their relationship with you?

Offer information freely

Another way to get a parent to ask fewer questions is to offer information on your own. Your parents are less likely to be worried about you if they know who your friends are, hear about what you get up to and know what you're feeling about certain things. Telling them in your own time and in your own way puts the control of information in your hands. Learning to communicate like this also has a major advantage in that it helps prepare you for handling a relationship. Get used to the passing of information and your communication within your friendships and relationships will improve.

- Tell them where you are going and why – they want to know because they are worried, not because they're being nosy.
- Let them into your life by introducing your friends – this way they will see they have nothing to worry about.
- Explain what's going on at school – so they don't imagine the worst.

Don't let them assume the worst

As tempting as it is to wind your parents up and make them think you're sexually active when you're not, or that you're out causing havoc when you're round at a friend's house, resist the urge. Letting them assume that you know more than you do (or are doing all the things they don't want you to do) will have a bad knock-on effect for you. First, it will encourage your parents to clamp down on you because they don't trust you; second, it may cause them to take radical action, such as removing you from your friends; and third, it could lead to your relationship with them self-destructing. If you're angry because they are assuming things that aren't true, such as that you're having sex, or you're hiding something, do the following:

- Put them straight – without being defensive.
- Ask them why they don't trust you and evaluate if they are being reasonable or not.
- Set up boundaries together that can build trust, such as calling when you're going to be late, or a weekday curfew.

Spark discussion when you're concerned

Sex education is an ever-changing subject and you're likely to come across new information faster than your parents will – which is why it pays to spark discussion with your parents so that they stay as up to date as you and can help you unravel the confusing bits. For instance, you may learn something in your PSHE lessons that your parents won't yet have heard of; or you may feel under pressure by a sex rumour that's going round at school; or maybe you feel angry about the way a friend is being treated over a sexual revelation. Use these as discussion points with your parents, as talking to them can help you find ways to deal with the areas you feel are confusing or tricky.

- Talk about the double standards you experience and see what help they can offer you.
- Discuss new information that comes your way.
- Focus on the emotional aspects of sex as much as the physical.

Self-esteem and sex

If your parents are always banging on about self-esteem and you're bored by it, here's why it's so important when it comes to sex. The fact is, we are all very exposed to heartbreak when it comes to forming relationships and falling in love, and if you're someone who doesn't feel good enough or feels weak and powerless in dealing with others, you're at a higher risk of making bad sexual choices and ending up in an unhealthy relationship. If on the other hand you have high self-esteem, you'll be less likely to tolerate anything but the best from your friends and partners – meaning it pays in the love and sex stakes to have high self-worth.

Bump up your quota and it will help you to:

- Like yourself and so expect more from your partners.
- Feel strong so you won't be taken advantage of in a relationship.
- Get out of a bad relationship as quickly as possible.
- Not have sex in order to be liked.
- Not mistake sex for love.
- Not feel pressurized into having sex.

The dictionary definition of self-esteem is having a good opinion of yourself, so a quick test is to ask yourself, 'Do I like who I am?'

If it's a resounding no with a thousand reasons why, you need self-esteem. The good news is that self-esteem can be learnt. Just as we learn to give ourselves a hard time for not looking good or not saying the right thing, we can learn to give ourselves a break and actually like who we are so that we don't have to value ourselves in terms of things like sex or possessions or acclaim.

Of course it's easy to say boost your self-esteem, but doing it's another matter entirely. The best way to feel good about yourself is to work out what you do and don't like about yourself, what your talents are and what you're good at. If nothing comes to mind, ask your best friends for help and work out what it is that makes you a good friend, a good person and a good son or daughter. Are you, for instance, someone who's good at making others laugh, or a good listener, or someone who brings out the best in others? Are you good at sport, spotting new trends, or clever with words or music? Remember a talent is a flair for something you're good at – not necessarily something that wins you academic acclaim or sports prizes or even approving looks from the opposite sex. Here are some other ways to boost your self-esteem.

Learn to face the things that scare you
I'm not talking naked bungee jumping but simply the small things that make you feel freaked out – such as talking to someone who makes you nervous; answering questions in class; telling someone you don't understand something;

and/or doing a sport you feel afraid of. Try building what the experts call a 'personal fear pyramid'. This is a list of your personal fears from 1 to 10, with 1 being your biggest fear and 10 being your smallest anxiety. When you have your list, you start at number 10 and work your way through them all (your aim isn't to get to your biggest fear but to increase your belief in what you're capable of facing).

Conquering your fears like this is a very powerful exercise because it enables you to see that you have power and inner strength and aren't at the mercy of people stronger, bigger, older or more assertive than you.

Listen to yourself

Think you have nothing to offer the world? Well, think of all the times you knew you were right but didn't say so until it was too late. Boosting your self-belief is all about getting used to your gut feeling and learning to trust yourself. If you can put your own self-belief against that of others, you'll know how to cope when a situation feels wrong for you – i.e. if your friends are trying to persuade you that everyone's having sex, you can make up your own mind and do what feels right for you.

Talk about what's bothering you

Most of the problems that come into magazine advice pages about sex and love are to do with people bottling up their feelings and fears, and not telling anyone what's bothering them. If you hide your true feelings all that will happen is you'll start to believe no-one understands you, and you'll be right. To be understood you need to let people in to see what's going on.

Take responsibility

Your relationship with your parents sucks, you hate school, no-one wants to date you and your life is rubbish – and let's face it, it's everyone else's fault but your own. Instead of taking responsibility, most of us kid ourselves that we have no choice or control over our lives, which leads us to make decisions that we can later come to regret. Taking responsibility means taking control of your life, facing up to your negative views of yourself and working on your good points so that no matter what happens you are never at the mercy of others.

Be who you are

Think about the personas you present to the world. The person you are in your head, at home, at school, with your friends and with girlfriends/boyfriends – which one is the one most like you? Which one do you like best and why? Which one would you like to be all the time? You don't have to live up to the expectations of friends and family, or even of girl-friends/boyfriends – you just have to live up to your own!

'I got very good sex education because it was never made a big deal of in my home. We talked about it and it was open and I always knew I could talk to mum because I was close to her, but at the same time she really respected my own privacy and let me come to her.'

ANNA MARTINEZ, Sex Education Forum

'I didn't have any sex education. I went to an Irish Catholic Christian Brothers school, and I suppose I would have to say I am lucky enough not to have any negative experiences from that education. As you can imagine, there was absolutely never, ever any discussion about sexual issues or relationship issues. What on earth could these celibate men, who spent years in an all-male seminary and then an all-male school, have taught us? Luckily, we had some lay teachers as well who had some experience of the world and there was some discussion on very, very rare occasions when issues came up in a novel that we would be studying.

In the end I got my sex education from pals and furtively looking up books and dictionaries. I got nothing from adults. My mum, in fairness, did try once, but I hadn't a notion what she was talking about. I was too embarrassed to pursue the issue with questions. It was only really when I went to university at seventeen and a half years of age that I had free access to excellent libraries and read about sex stuff, and even managed to find a copy of Masters and Johnson's book on Sexual Response which began to broaden my understanding.'

DR COLM O'MAHONY

YOUR QUESTIONS ANSWERED

Q I'm worried that if my ten- and twelve-year-olds learn about sex they'll go out there and do it. Why can't we keep kids innocent?

A To keep all sexual information away from a child you'd probably have to ban all contact with the outside world. Don't be fooled – even if your child is not talking about sex, he or she already has some idea of what it's all about, thanks to TV, videos, films and friends. The longer you avoid the subject at home, the longer your child will have to build up an inaccurate picture of sex. As for sex education encouraging kids to have sex, there is no evidence to prove this (plus, let's face it, talking about something does not make a child rush out and do it – think about anti-drugs talks for example). In any case, sex education is not just about the mechanics of sex but, more importantly, how to avoid abuse and peer pressure, and how to make informed choices that will protect their health.

Q My fourteen-year-old son cringes whenever sex happens on the TV or a person gets naked. Is this a sign that he's not ready to discuss sex with me?

A No – it's a sign that he is ready to talk about it. His discomfort indicates that perhaps sex isn't such an open topic in your house and so he feels acute embarrassment when it happens in front of you, imagining that you are also embarrassed about witnessing it with him. The next time it happens, make a comment about what you're watching that sparks a discussion. He may not respond, but if you keep making comments you can build towards asking him questions that will help you to determine his level of understanding and what he needs to know.

Q We're about to have the sex-education talk in our house – should my husband and I talk to our daughters (aged nine and thirteen years) together about sex or should I do it?

A In an ideal world input from both parents from an early age is best; however, if you're going straight in to talk about it for the first time, be wary of doing it together. Your girls will not hear your message if they are more focused on how uncomfortable it is to have their dad sitting there! Plus, if this is new to them, it may be awkward for them to ask questions. Start slowly by talking to them about the basics and then begin to introduce discussion on sex and relationships in a less formal way with your husband around. This way they'll gradually get the message that it's fine to be open with both of you.

Q Sex is an off-limits conversation in our house and whenever I try to bring it up my parents jump down my throat and assume I am having sex. I can't talk to them about anything as they are anti-sex-before-marriage, anti-abortion and anti-homosexuality. I don't feel the same way. Where can I go for information?

A Sometimes parental morals due to religious or cultural views do get in the way of sex education. If you feel you need to talk about issues with someone you trust because you can't do it at home, check out the Resources section at the back of the book for confidential agencies, helplines and websites that can give you a wider view of the world.

Q **My fifteen-year-old daughter just told me she has had sex – I feel shocked. Have I left it too late to talk to her about sex?**

A It's never too late to start talking about sex. Your daughter may have had sex, but her sexual knowledge may well be limited. Is she using contraception, practising safe sex and/or is she happy with her decision to have sex? You need to find out all of the above and also why she decided she was ready to have sex, as she may need your support and advice more than ever.

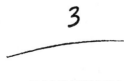

PUBERTY

I DON'T REMEMBER WHERE I GOT MY SEX EDUCATION FROM, which is pretty much a sign that I probably didn't get much. At some stage I realized girls got their periods and boys were obviously different, but it wasn't until I became a parent that I found my views on sex and relationships challenged and realized that the common view – 'Well, I didn't get any but I survived' – just wasn't good enough. I now think that for sex and relationship education to be successful, we all need to do it together and on a repetitive basis so that all the information sticks, and so that kids not only know what's happening to them when something changes overnight but they also know whom to turn to.

If you're not convinced about the necessity of starting with the basics, think about your own puberty years and the pain and horror of pulsating spots, untimely sexual urges, and burgeoning (or not) body parts. Then try to remember how you coped and add into the mix some of the careless things adults probably threw your way – things such as 'You're a bit spotty aren't you?'; 'Wow, you're getting big/you're a bit small'; 'Oh, what are those then [pointing to some new growing body part]?' – and recall how you felt.

Of course, being the caring, sharing kind of parent, you're probably never going to do that and your kids are going to sail through puberty with not even the hint of a mood swing thanks to your considerate approach. In an ideal world this, of course, would be true, but unfortunately even the most skilful parent has to consider that they will have no control over their children's raging hormones. Growth spurts, body changes, spots and body hair aside, puberty and its whole range of emotions are going to be felt right across your family.

Daunting as I am making it sound, puberty is not the end of the world for anyone. It's a fantastic and thrilling time; it means your children are growing up, can do more for themselves and won't need you as much on a day-to-day basis (apart from the 2am I-need-a-lift-home calls).

As Dr Colm O'Mahony says:

'Young people develop at different rates and what suits one individual at a certain age would be unsuitable for another. So a great deal of flexibility is needed when it comes to puberty talks, but in general I think teenagers from the age of thirteen upwards (at an earlier age, say ten or younger, the mechanics of puberty can be explained) should have a good knowledge of sexual issues, sexually transmitted infections, relationships, self-esteem and should be able to enact scenarios of negotiating no sex or safer sex, with the confidence to delay sex until they are ready.'

So here's how to avoid the nudge, nudge, wink, wink approach to sex and puberty we Brits are so good at and do it the right way.

WHAT IS PUBERTY?

 Puberty is essentially the term given for the body's natural progression from a child-like physique to an adult body. In boys, it usually begins between nine and fourteen years of age and in girls between eight and thirteen, though of late statistics do show more kids are hitting the younger end of the scale and starting puberty before their parents have twigged what's going on.

When your children will start is hard to say, which is why it's vital to begin preparing them before they show signs. The good news is that children notice the difference in their bodies and yours from a young age and will willingly ask you embarrassing questions about body parts until the day your tone of voice silences them. As embarrassing as it is to have a small child highlight the size of your breasts (or someone else's) in public or inform your friends that 'Dad has a penis' – use these instances to talk to them about their bodies and what will happen as they grow older.

When talking to pre-teens about puberty the most important thing to emphasize is that it's not a race, even though it feels that way at school. Messages to get across include:

- Puberty is a process that can take as long as six years to even out, but it *will* end.

- Everyone matures at their own pace, but eventually we all catch up, so just because all your daughter's friends have bras or their periods and all your son's friends have deep voices and facial hair it doesn't mean they never will.
- The changes will not occur on a strict timeline.
- Puberty isn't a sign that you're emotionally ready to have sex, it is simply that your body has matured.

Of course it's not always easy to bring up things like periods, breasts and untimely erections with an eight-year-old, who (a) will think it's hysterical and (b) will be embarrassed. If this is your first sex and relationships talk, come prepared with books, diagrams and answers to non-obvious questions such as 'Did that happen to you and how did it feel?' And remember, if you're stuck for a reply, honesty and simplicity always work best. Also, don't be afraid to admit to not knowing answers and if you're really stuck use it as an opportunity to suggest you look queries up together on the internet. Again, avoid trying to get a large amount of information across all at once. The facts of puberty can be dry and medical, so your children are likely to switch off if you drone on about ovaries, growth spurts and hormones without filling in the more exciting bits, like sexual feelings and looking older. Good questions to ask ten-year-olds and under before launching into the whole subject are:

- Where do babies come from?
- Have you heard the word period/sex, etc., and what do you think it means?

- What do you think is going to happen to your body as you get older?
- Have you noticed any changes in your friends' bodies?

Questions for ten-year-olds and over:
- Is there anything that you'd like to ask me about your body or boys/girls and their bodies?
- What are your friends saying about boys/girls/periods/sex?
- Do you find anything scary or worrying about puberty?
- Do you know where to go for help if you don't want to ask me?

It also pays to be prepared to relate questions back to yourself and your own body, as this will make it much more interesting. What child doesn't want to hear about the embarrassing time you woke up with a spot the size of China on the end of your nose or how you embarrassed yourself when you first asked someone out? In terms of who gets to do the talking in your house, it really depends on you and your child. While it's been shown that girls who can talk to their fathers create better relationships later on with men, the truth is that most girls would rather run down the road naked than talk to their fathers about periods and most fathers definitely do not want to talk to their girls about body changes and sex. However, that's not to say fathers can't offer sex and relationship education: they can be a fantastic source of information about boys for their daughters (though you may first have to squash your 'I-must-protect-my-daughter-at-all-costs' instinct!) and a good source of how to deal with girls for their boys. If you're a single dad, don't despair – you can do just as good a job as a single mum, as long as you keep the lines of communication open from the beginning. If you just can't face certain areas, or your child can't, try the open-book technique talked about in Chapter 2.

By far the best way to start your family talks is to allow all questions to be asked and answered (in an age-appropriate way) by both parents. This will create a base of understanding so that when you get more specific, your child will know that both of you are available for help and comment if need be. In reality a child will usually choose the parent he or she feels more comfortable with, so you don't have to try to force them to talk to one of you (or both of you).

If you are the primary information giver, do try to draw the other parent in on the more appropriate questions. For instance, if you're talking about erections and your child asks, 'Does it hurt when men get erections?', you could say, 'No, it doesn't, does it X?' Also bear in mind that, while the biological information on puberty is taught at school, discussion with both sexes on the emotional aspects of puberty is limited and in some areas distinctly lacking. Really to understand the information they are being taught at school, your kids need to be able to discuss what puberty means for them, and query the parts they don't understand (and are too afraid to admit to their friends). This means trying never to be shocked by what your children ask you. It's near on impossible as a parent, but you've got to try to bite the bullet so that they keep asking. And don't worry if you think you're telling them something they already know, or even if they just say they know it as a way of getting you to stop talking. The more you repeat sex and relationship information, the better the chance it will sink in.

RAGING HORMONES

It's difficult to know where to start with puberty, which is why talking about hormones can help your children understand why body changes are happening.

 The Science Bit... Explain that hormones are the brain's chemical messengers, which are released in conjunction with the body's time clock to start sexual maturity and growth, and that this process happens in three ways:

- The first bit involves the release of hormones that activate the ovaries and testes to mature. Then begins the production of high levels of sex hormones – oestrogen in girls and testosterone in boys. These sex hormones cause changes that result in fertility – meaning periods will begin in girls, and sperm production in boys.
- The second bit centres on the release of testosterone-like hormones in both sexes and contributes to acne and facial hair, as well as the development of pubic and underarm hair.
- The third bit involves the growth hormone (GH), which causes rapid physical growth.

With all this going on, the body starts to get longer, bigger and wider. Some teenagers may find themselves with growing pains (aching limbs) and may experience rapid growth spurts that leave them with stretch marks on their hips, backs and stomachs. As the body grows taller, it will also gain weight.

Boys will find their shoulders widening and their bodies becoming more muscular. Girls will become curvier and will notice an increase in overall body fat to aid their fertility (body fat is essential for the production of oestrogen). The ebb and flow of these hormones will also trigger the more tempestuous emotional changes, such as tearfulness, anger, frustration and erratic mood swings.

You may find your kids become overly sensitive and nothing you say is right, or they may become sad and blue for no reason. In most cases their emotions will level out; however, in extreme cases, if your child appears depressed and overly anxious about the changes he or she is going through, a doctor's view should be sought.

When it comes to helping your son or daughter deal with their hormones, two lifestyle habits that will help are sufficient sleep and good nutrition. If your kids skip breakfast, eat fast food for lunch and dinner, plus stay up later, their hormones are going to ricochet between highs and lows, and they're going to feel bad and get cranky. A healthy diet is essential as their body is demanding more fuel in order to grow, and more sleep is vital so they can cope with the changes.

Emotionally, your teenagers need to know that you understand why their moods are so erratic and why they are experiencing a drop in self-esteem, but at the same time lay down guidelines and boundaries for behaviour (rather than giving them excuses to act out) so they don't feel they are spiralling out of control.

PUBERTY AND BOYS

What happens to boys?

- The penis and scrotum get larger around twelve years old.
- A growth spurt between thirteen and fourteen years old (on average).
- The testicles (balls) become sensitive.
- They experience frequent erections.
- They experience ejaculations and 'wet dreams'.
- They start to masturbate.
- They develop larger muscles and broader shoulders.

For boys, ejaculation – the release of semen (cum) through the penis – is one of the first signs that they are going through puberty. Ejaculation may occur because of a wet dream, which is a sexual dream where ejaculation occurs involuntarily while a boy is sleeping, or through masturbation (though your teenager may not realize that this is what he is doing), so the chances are you may not know puberty has started unless your son is forthcoming with information. To help him see that wet dreams and masturbation are normal, you need to talk to him about sexual arousal, sexual feelings and even masturbation.

Excruciating as the thought of talking about this may be, it's essential if you want your children to enter adulthood with a healthy attitude to sex, rather than feeling shame and disgust at their own sexual pleasure.

Ways to discuss the above are to:

- Ask them what they already know/have heard about wet dreams and masturbation.
- Talk about the subject in the third person – e.g. 'I know X said he had a wet dream but didn't know what it was.'
- Ask which parent they'd prefer to discuss this with and/ or what information you can help them with.

The first physical change that a boy might notice is the enlargement of the testes and the lengthening of his penis. This will be followed by an increased amount of pubic hair that is noticeably coarser and darker than before. It is at this point that the 'growth spurt' usually begins and the more obvious physical changes happen, including a gain in muscle mass, the voice deepening, and acne. Because puberty is a complex period of growth, reassurance about what is normal is important.

Emphasize that:

- Disparities in height, muscles and weight are normal – use magazine pictures of adults to highlight this.
- Acne, while normal, is treatable – check out the Acne Support Group website (see Resources) for information.
- Penis size is not an indication of how good you're going to be at sex – this is an ideal way to start discussing sexual myths.

Here are some changes to talk about with your son.

Voice changes

At puberty the larynx (or voice box) enlarges and the muscles or vocal cords grow; this causes the voice to change (also known as 'break'). At times the voice will ricochet unexpectedly between highs and lows, but this will even out to a deeper adult tone.

Wet dreams

Damp PJs and sheets usually equal a wet dream caused by an ejaculation, not urination, and are to do with having an arousing dream. This phenomenon needs to be explained to boys so they don't think they are wetting the bed or worry that something is wrong with them. Reassurance also needs to be given that they cannot prevent it from happening.

Involuntary erections

Also known as spontaneous erections, untimely erections or downright annoying erections. Unfortunately, you need to explain that the penis will get harder and larger at certain times without it being touched and without having any sexual thoughts. These involuntary erections can be really embarrassing and mortifying, especially if they occur in public. Again, explain to your son that they are normal and are a sign that his body is working properly. Suggest helpful ways to make them go down, such as thinking about a person he dislikes, or imagining someone unattractive trying to kiss him. The good news is that involuntary erections eventually go away for good.

Breast enlargement

Many boys also experience swelling of the breasts during the early years of puberty and the breasts may also feel tender or even painful. This is called pubertal gynecomastia and is due to hormonal surges; it does not mean your horrified teen will get breasts and it will subside. See your GP if your son is worried.

Body hair

Body hair really gets going during puberty. Some boys will start to notice hair growing in tufts on their face and around the chin, on the cheeks and above the lip. Also, hair grows on the chest, the armpits and in the pubic region. Boys don't really need to do anything about this new hair until it gets thick, when they will want to talk with their parents about shaving.

Sexual urges

Testosterone is the male sexual hormone and men carry around twenty to forty times as much of it as women do. Testosterone happens to be extremely sensitive to its environment. For the teenage boy this means sexual arousal is potentially around every corner, so don't be amazed if your son starts getting more embarrassed around girls or while watching TV.

Ways to deal with his hormone-induced moods

- Don't criticize him when he's down in the dumps, as his testosterone levels will plummet, leaving you with a surly, depressed human doormat.
- Let him help himself. Don't be put off if he masturbates a lot – this kick-starts testosterone and gets rid of stress.
- Get him moving. Taking regular exercise not only promotes the production of all the body's hormones but helps keep his moods level.

It's also worth noting that boys in particular become interested in pornography around this age (though some girls do as well, simply because the material is sexually stimulating and not because they are gay). While it's tempting to go mad when you find porn in their room and/or lecture them on respecting the female body and the politics of pornography, bear in mind that it's curiosity that's pushing them in this direction. Go crazy and you're going to make them feel 'dirty'. Instead you need to talk to them about:

- The nature of the pictures they are looking at, and why you maybe don't approve. Talk about how viewing explicit images can desensitize people and affect their view of women and sex.
- How looking at porn can have a negative effect, leading to expectations that are neither realistic nor healthy.
- How curiosity is normal but obsessive behaviour around pornography is not.

Aggression

While anger isn't the domain of teenage boys only, many boys do feel surges of aggression and lash out during puberty. Part of this is down to hormones, but much of it has to do with the natural frustration that comes with being a teenager. This is why discussion of behaviour and the way you expect people to behave towards you is needed. A good way to talk about it is to:

- Admit that everyone gets angry (after all, much of how your child has learnt to display his anger has been learnt from you) and tactics that can be used to control anger such as counting to ten before reacting and/or taking time out in the middle of an argument.
- Ask your child what pressures (if any) he feels you may be placing on his shoulders, or what teachers are nagging him about at school.
- Find ways he can express his angry feelings to stop him lashing out. An objective person such as a counsellor may be of good use here, or the use of an anger diary that's for his eyes only.

- Find ways to reduce frustration and stress, such as sport, more sleep, a better diet and getting him to pinpoint what needs to change in order for him to feel better.
- At the same time, ensure there are boundaries for behaviour so that he learns there are repercussions for not controlling angry feelings.

Girls, periods and pregnancy

Sooner or later your son will have a relationship. If it's with a girl it pays for him to understand how the female body works, not just in order to have a good relationship but also to understand how a pregnancy happens. To help him you need to explain periods and to have talks about girls with him. For information on this, see the 'Periods' section.

'I knew nothing about puberty. I had no idea what was happening. To my eternal embarrassment, I didn't know what a wet dream was until I suddenly had one one night and nearly died of shock. I also wish I'd known about girls developing through puberty as well and periods and all that stuff. Like most men of my day, our first sexual experiences were unprotected and could easily have been a lifelong disaster.'

DR COLM O'MAHONY

THE OTHER SIDE OF THE COIN
Biology Basics – The Male Anatomy Map

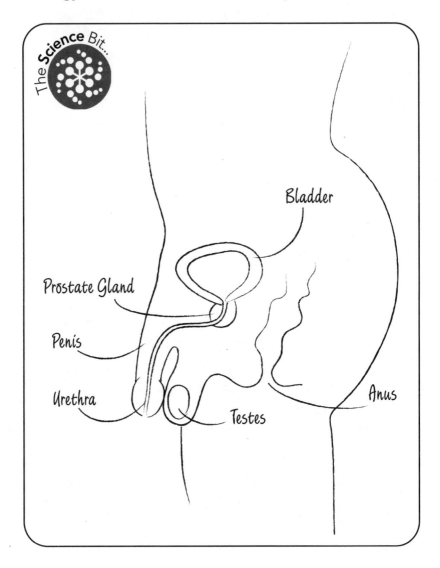

The Science Bit...

Bladder

Prostate Gland

Penis

Urethra

Testes

Anus

Penis

 Made up of spongy erectile tissue, involuntary muscle, nerves and blood vessels – the penis is more than a simple shaft-shaped organ that hangs partly outside the body. The head of the penis (or glans) is highly sensitive and at the centre of it is the external urethral opening, through which semen and urine are ejaculated. Most penises are on average 9 centimetres long when flaccid (soft) but any size penis is able to become erect. While soft, penises look very different; when erect all penises average somewhere between 12.5 and 17.5 centimetres long.

At some point you might worry about the size of your penis and compare yourself to others with a shifty look in the changing room. To put your mind at rest, the size of a penis when flaccid has no bearing on how big it will be when erect – so don't worry.

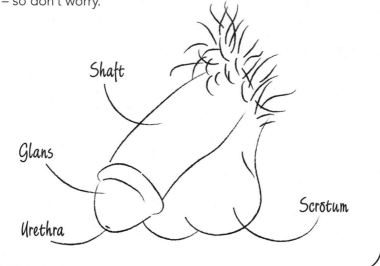

Shaft

Glans

Urethra

Scrotum

Urethra

 This runs from the bladder to the end of the penis and carries both semen and urine.

You may wonder if you'll wee as you ejaculate (release semen from the penis) and the answer is no. The urethra cannot carry semen and urine at the same time. During sex, a muscle in the bladder clamps shut, preventing a flow of urine on ejaculation.

Foreskin

 This is the skin that covers the penis and is folded over the glans. Some boys have this skin removed for religious or health reasons during childhood; this is known as circumcision and means the head of the penis is permanently exposed.

Circumcision doesn't affect sex, nor is it cleaner than being uncircumcised,* as long as you wash under the foreskin. This last point is essential, as a thick secretion known as smegma may accumulate under the foreskin and if it's not washed away it will begin to smell and an infection may occur.

---

*A study on circumcision from the University of Chicago found there were no significant sexual health differences between circumcised and uncircumcised men.

Testicles

The Science Bit... These are two small glands found below your penis. The testes produce millions of sperm every day and hang away from the body because sperm needs to be produced at a temperature 5 degrees lower than the body's normal temperature of 98.6°F (36°C). Usually the left testicle hangs slightly lower than the right to prevent them colliding. The testes also produce and secrete the male sex hormone testosterone.

One thing you should be aware of here is the subject of blue balls. Balls do not need sexual relief when excited and guys who tell girls this are just trying to pull a fast one. The reality is, while the testes do fill with blood and sexual tension and feel uncomfortable, relief is not needed to make the feeling go away.

The other fact about testicles that needs to be passed on is the risk of testicular cancer. This is the most common cancer in men aged fifteen to thirty-four. The number of men diagnosed with this cancer has doubled in the last twenty-five years, with around 2,000 new cases every year. The good news is that over 95 per cent of men who seek treatment in the early stages are cured. The crucial thing is to get treatment as early as possible, meaning get to know your testicles, examine them regularly for what's normal and what isn't, and if you notice a change (which in most cases won't be cancer) see your doctor as soon as possible (see Resources for more on this).

Scrotum

 This is the pouch of skin that contains the testicles. It's baggy to enable the testes to hang away from the body (see Testicles). While the scrotum looks like one sac, it's actually divided into two areas to house each testicle separately.

Prostate gland

 This lies inside your body below the bladder and makes 30 per cent of the fluid contained in semen. It's about the size of a walnut.

Semen

 Semen is a mixture of fluid and sperm that is ejected from the penis during ejaculation. It's made up of 10 per cent sperm and 90 per cent of fluids (60 per cent from the seminal vesicles and 30 per cent from the prostate gland). On ejaculation, the average amount ejected is usually about one teaspoonful.

Sperm

 The Science Bit... Sperm, or spermatozoa, are the wriggly tadpole things that are in fact male cells that need to unite with female eggs through sex to make a baby. The biological purpose of sperm is to transport genetic information from the male body to the female.

The average man produces sperm at a rate of about 1,000 every second and up to 30 billion each month – 50–100 million can be found in one teaspoon of semen (though 40 per cent will be of no use).

The reason why sperm are produced in such large numbers is because they are fairly fragile, easily destroyed by hot temperatures (don't wear your jeans too tight) and alien environments (the female vagina). This means that even though around 100 million are dispersed in one ejaculation during sex, only around fifty get close to the female egg (don't take any comfort in this though – it only takes one and teenage sperm are like bionic swimmers when it comes to fertilizing an egg).

PUBERTY AND GIRLS

What happens to girls?

- Breasts begin to grow between seven and thirteen years old (on average).
- Periods begin approximately two years after this (nine–fifteen years).
- Girls gain body fat and become curvier.
- They experience a growth spurt.
- They experience sexual urges.
- Some start to masturbate.

If you think the male sex hormone is bad news at puberty, take a look at the female one. Oestrogen is the sex kitten of female hormones – sexy, vivacious and desperate for attention – and the very culprit that will transform your girl into a teenager. The first sign that oestrogen is surging is the arrival of the first menstrual period approximately twelve months to two years after the breasts start to develop. From this point on her breasts will get larger, hips rounder and body hair will start to grow under the arms and in the pubic area. It means that before this your pre-teen will be turning into a woman and will need more than what school is offering her. As Dionne, aged sixteen, says, 'Sex education at my school was absolutely rubbish – they just mentioned body parts like your ovaries but didn't talk about how you might feel about sex or about contraception.'

Periods

Periods, menstruation, being on the blob, the curse – the list of ways to say you're on is endless, and even if your daughter hasn't started yet it's likely she's already picked up how women talk about periods. If you think back to when you started, you may remember what a dilemma periods were. Half of you probably wanted to start so that you weren't the last in your group and the other half probably dreaded the very thought. Read any teen advice page and you'll see nothing much has changed – which is where you need to come in. Dispelling myths, pointing out the obvious (which may not be obvious to your daughter) and helping her through the anxieties of starting her periods is where you can help.

Be aware that how you discuss periods will instill in your daughter how she'll feel about them. Concentrate on the negatives, such as PMS, period pains and the annoyance of the bleeding itself, and she'll not only dread it but will go through life regarding her periods as a hindrance rather than a sign her body is healthy and working properly. Of course this doesn't mean you have to pretend to be ecstatically happy about periods (she won't believe you anyway), but try to be positive about what to expect.

As most girls will have their first period (known as the menarche) when they reach 48kg (7$\frac{1}{2}$ stone), which will usually be between the ages of eleven and fourteen, it's essential to start your talks about periods well before this. It means discussing how periods work and why they happen from around the age of eight. The best way to do this is to keep your talk clear and simple. Start by asking what your child knows about periods so you have an idea of where she is and what information needs to be given and/or corrected. Below are some common questions your daughter may ask and some answers to put her mind at rest.

THE OTHER SIDE OF THE COIN
Period Questions and Answers

What is a period?

 A period is another name for menstruation and it happens every month as the body starts to prepare itself for a possible pregnancy. Two weeks before your period starts, an egg is released from one of your ovaries (the place where eggs are kept) and travels down the fallopian tubes to the uterus (or womb, where later in life a baby will grow). While this is happening (usually a two- or three-day process) the uterus prepares for the egg's arrival by lining its walls with extra tissue – a bit like making a nest. If the egg is then not fertilized – i.e. you haven't had unprotected sex and a sperm hasn't united with an egg – this lining has no use, so it breaks down and is ejected by the body as a period. Therefore your period is a mixture of blood, tissue lining and fluid.

Does this mean I'm ready to have sex?

In the same way that learning to walk as a toddler doesn't mean you're ready to run a marathon, starting your periods doesn't mean you are ready to have sex. Periods are only a sign that your body is now capable of making a baby. This is a very different thing from feeling ready for sex, which tends to happen much later when you meet someone you love and have a relationship.

Will it hurt?

Some women feel uncomfortable and/or have cramp-like pains when they have their period. This is due to the way the body releases the lining of the womb. On the whole the pain is not bad, doesn't last very long and feels something like a stomach ache. When it occurs the best way to deal with it is to:

- Take a painkiller such as Ibuprofen – it will ease the cramps.
- Place a hot water bottle on your stomach to help relax the muscles.

Will blood gush out everywhere when I start?

No – you'll usually get a small sign of spotting (little drops of blood) or discharge (clear or brownish fluid) in your pants a few days before your period starts, or an aching feeling in your stomach. Even if you don't experience this, the blood you lose during a period is only two or three tablespoons, though it always looks like more.

THE MENSTRUAL MONTH

❄ **Days 1–7**

EXPECT TO FEEL...

You should be feeling relaxed, happy and calm. This is all down to the release of a hormone from the brain's pituitary gland called FSH (Follicle Stimulating Hormone). This hormone stimulates your ovaries and leads to the production of the female sex hormone, oestrogen.

❄ **Days 8–14**

EXPECT TO FEEL...

Thanks to high levels of oestrogen, you'll feel at your most confident and attractive right now.

❄ **Days 14–21**

EXPECT TO FEEL...

The brain will trigger ovulation. Post ovulation you'll feel some changes on the physical front: you might begin to notice some weight gain, especially around your breasts and stomach (the body begins to store water so you don't get dehydrated before your period arrives). You're also likely to feel flabby and low about yourself (PMS).

❄ **Days 21–28**

EXPECT TO FEEL...

Your concentration levels will be at an all-time low, and you're more likely to feel tired as your body's energies are channelled into other areas of your body to start your period.

How long will my period last?

Between five and seven days, though you won't bleed heavily all the time. You'll start off slowly, build up to more and then it will level off.

How do I work out when my next period is due?

 A period will happen approximately every twenty-eight days. This means you need to count forwards twenty-eight days from the first day you start bleeding. Bear in mind, though, that for the first two years periods are irregular and sometimes stop for months; this is because the ovaries are still maturing and so an egg isn't always released. Plus, be aware of how much your mood can influence your periods – get stressed and your body's time clock will be thrown off path.

Will other people be able to tell I am having a period?

No – because it's happening inside you. If they say they can, they are only winding you up.

What should I use, tampons or towels?

It's a matter of preference. Sanitary towels are thin pads made of a soft cotton-like material. Most towels have a sticky strip on them that sticks the pad to the inside of your knickers and then acts like a plaster to soak up the blood. They are easy to use and you'll know when to change them.

A tampon is like a small rolled-up piece of cotton wool with a string at one end. A girl pushes a tampon into her vagina, leaving the string hanging outside her body. The tampon soaks up the blood, ensuring nothing comes out, and the string is then used to pull the tampon out.

How do I know when to change a tampon?

A sanitary towel should be changed every three to four hours during the day, even if the flow of blood is not very great, and can be used overnight without changing. Tampons should also be changed several times a day and usually you'll know they need to be changed as you'll be aware of a slight tugging feeling as the tampon gets heavier.

What is PMS?

 Premenstrual syndrome is the name given to the host of symptoms you may get a week to ten days before your period. Some women suffer more than others with PMS and much of this is down to their hormones. If you feel tearful, moody and bloated before a period you can help yourself by cutting down on junk food (sugar makes PMS worse), by exercising (this releases feel-good hormones into your body) and by talking about your worries with a friend or parent.

Strong mood swings

Girls, more than boys, tend to suffer from erratic mood swings during puberty, which may cause your daughter to become over-sensitive, tearful and at times aggressive and self-destructive. It's a tantalizing mix, partly fuelled by fluctuating hormones but also by the strong emotions all teenagers and some pre-teens go through. The problem with things like anger, sadness and depression is that they are overwhelming emotions that can cause a child who doesn't understand what's happening to think everything is hopeless. Watch out for signs such as:

- A radical change in behaviour.
- Over-sleeping.
- Change in appetite.
- Signs of self-harm, like cutting themselves.
- Negative language about themselves.
- Unexplained crying.
- Cutting themselves off from friends.
- Change in behaviour at school.

If any of the above persist, see your GP; but above all let your daughter know that she can come to you for help and advice no matter what, and also make sure she knows where she can go outside the home if she feels desperate, lonely or in need of support (see Resources).

Crushes

It's easy for admiration to turn to attraction, especially with pre-teens and teenage girls, who, thanks to their rampant hormones, may suddenly feel they are in love with someone they don't know very well. For many of them it's a practice run for a real relationship and a way for them to examine their feelings and run through the highs and lows of falling in love within the safety of their minds (go on, admit it – we've all done it).

Don't be fooled, however: it may not be real to you, but the highs and lows are real enough for your daughter. This means you need to talk to her about it, especially since she may have fallen for someone who is exploiting her inexperience.

It's especially important to know with whom your child spends time, in terms of older children and adults, and watch for warning signs that grooming may be taking place. If you think a child is being groomed (i.e. persuaded to trust someone who has ulterior motives), trust your feelings and act on them:

- Listen for statements or questions from your daughter that would sound suspicious.
- Encourage your daughter to tell you more about the time she spends with the person.
- Give your child the prevention tools to help identify inappropriate behaviour, such as being made to look at things she doesn't want to see, being made to touch someone or read sexually suggestive emails.
- Make sure your daughter understands that she can and should say no to anyone who makes her feel uncomfortable.

Weight gain

As weight is an issue for many girls, it pays to be positive when you start talking about this change. Try to emphasize that a certain amount of weight gain is required for energy, and that women need it even more to be fertile (body fat is needed for oestrogen to be produced). For this reason, around

25 per cent of the female adult body is fat while only 15 per cent of the male adult body is fat.

For both sexes, weight gain consists of fat, muscle, bone and organs (not just fat) and weight gain often happens before a height spurt. So try to avoid drawing attention to what's happening, unless your child is concerned, and don't start panicking if the weight seems to be well proportioned.

Unfortunately, with puberty, the desire for acceptance often leads to constant comparisons and judgements about what look is 'normal'.

The good news is that talking about puberty and its body changes helps girls to feel prepared for what's about to happen to them. To help them understand body image and how it affects their self-esteem and choices:

- Back up your practical information with messages and conversations about how there are many different body types that are considered beautiful.
- Again, use magazines and TV as an example of this, as well as encouraging your child to look around and witness it for herself.
- Finally, keep the focus off dieting and on being healthy. Keep your daughter active and encourage healthy eating practices which give her a little bit of what she likes alongside what's good for her.

BIOLOGY BASICS
The Female Anatomy Map

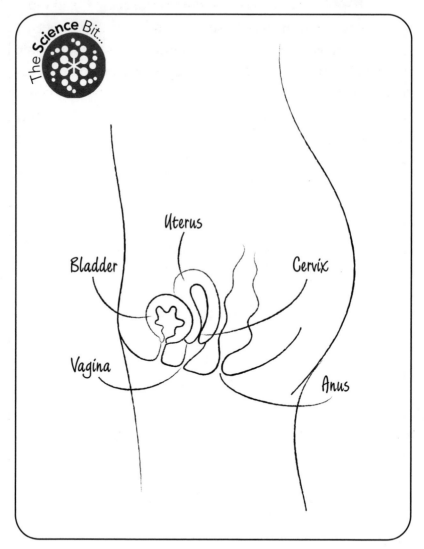

Vagina

The Science Bit... The vagina is literally the inside part of the female sex organs and is a soft, muscle-bound canal measuring about 7.5–10 centimetres. It has a variety of purposes. First, it's made for penetration by a penis during sex (and a tampon during a period); second, it serves as a birth canal for a baby; and third, it's the outlet for menstrual blood. At rest, the spongy muscle-bound walls of the vagina lie flat against each other, but during birth and sex the walls can stretch and then spring back together afterwards.

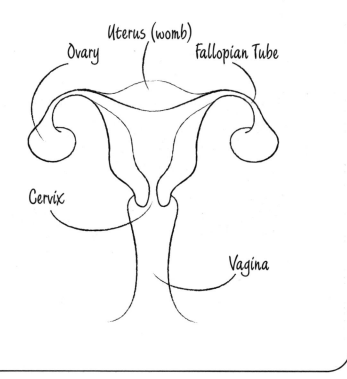

Ovary

Uterus (womb)

Fallopian Tube

Cervix

Vagina

Uterus

 This is the womb – where a developing foetus lives during pregnancy. It's about 7.5 centimetres long and 7.5 centimetres wide and has incredibly powerful muscles, which when they contract cause period pains and the contractions during pregnancy. During your menstrual cycle this is where the lining builds up and then breaks down to be released as a period.

Cervix

 This is also known as the neck of the womb (uterus); it is located at the top of the vagina and leads to the womb. It's a small, narrow area, about 2.5 centimetres long, and is made of very tough tissue. In the centre of this area is a small opening that allows sperm to get in and menstrual blood to flow out. This is also the area that remains closed during pregnancy and then dilates to allow the baby to come out. The cervix, though made of strong muscle and tissue, is however also a 'weak' area of the body because during unprotected sex two types of cells meet here (male and female) and this can cause the cells of the cervix to change (see Chapter 6).

Hymen

The hymen is the thin membrane of tissue that partly covers the entrance to the vagina. It has a small central perforation through which menstrual blood can flow. The hymen is the piece of tissue that is supposed to symbolize virginity. The fact is, it's just a thin membrane and some girls have it and some girls don't. In fact there is some new research from Holland that suggests the hymen doesn't exist at all and that it's a medical myth!

Vulva

An anatomically correct term that only doctors use to describe the external female sex organs. Basically speaking, this is the area of your genitalia which you can see if you peer at yourself with a mirror. It includes the mons pubis, the labia majora and labia minora (outer and inner lips) and the clitoris.

Mons pubis: the fatty padded area of skin that lies over the pubic bone, where all your pubic hair grows. You can find it about 10 centimetres below your belly button.

Labia majora: the vaginal lips – the two folds of skin that overlap your vaginal opening.

Labia minora: the small folds of skin found inside the labia majora. In some women they hang down, or protrude, from the labia majora, and in others they remain hidden in the outer folds.

Clitoris

The Science Bit... The clitoris is actually part of a much bigger organ – we're talking about 10 centimetres in length – that extends inside you and links to erectile tissue around the vagina. This small organ is the female equivalent of a man's penis, which basically means it comes with its own tiny shaft and glans and is even covered by a similar piece of skin to the foreskin, known as the hood. The sole purpose of this organ is to give you sexual pleasure.

To locate it go to the top of your vagina, where the two inner lips of the labia minora meet. It's worth noting that this whole area is also made of similar tissue to the penis, which is why it becomes erect on stimulation and why it feels good when rubbed. When flaccid (soft) the average clitoris is the size of a pine nut, and when aroused it swells to the size of a large peanut.

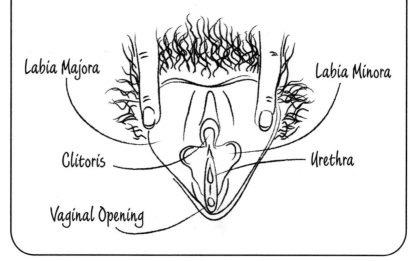

Breasts

The Science Bit... Small, large, lopsided, pert, droopy or flat – breasts are those spherical objects that all of us want until we get them. On a simple anatomical level, breasts are just fatty tissue with the only muscle in the whole area being the nipple. However, on the sexual front, the breasts, nipples and areola (pigmented area surrounding the nipple) are hugely sexually responsive to touch and alluring to the opposite sex.

It's important to realize that one breast often grows faster than the other and at a certain point this can make you seem lopsided, but they do end up roughly equal. Also, don't be fooled into thinking bigger is better. Thanks to the large amount of information there is out there on cosmetic surgery and the number of women who have breast enlargements, it's easy to get the idea that (a) to be attractive you have to have pert big breasts and (b) this is what men want. Bear in mind that bust size doesn't determine your attractiveness – you are more than your bra size!

AM I NORMAL?

As I pointed out in Chapter 2, feeling normal is something your children will worry about massively throughout puberty. Give them accurate and specific knowledge about what to expect and they're less likely to get anxious and upset, and more likely to come to you when they do have fears and worries. Besides growing sexual parts, periods and untimely erections, the following are other puberty hotspots that you need to talk about with your kids. You may think spots, weight problems and even shyness have little to do with sex and relationships, but they do, simply because all of them affect the way young people think about themselves. If one of these issues drags them down, their self-esteem dips, which in turn leads them to think less of themselves and make unhealthy choices.

Spots

The good news is, despite what you and your kids may have heard, spots and acne have nothing to do with eating chocolate and chips. Acne appears at puberty when the body's sebaceous (oil) glands over-produce. This then blocks up the skin pores, allowing bacteria to settle in and a big pustule to appear! The Acne Support Group charity says that all spots eventually clear up, but until then don't let your kids suffer in silence. Try topical spot treatments (available from the pharmacy) containing the active ingredients Benzoyl Peroxide or Azelaic acid and work on a two-month rule. If after eight weeks there's no marked improvement, try a new product; apply the same rule and then if that doesn't work see your GP. He or she can prescribe antibiotics that work directly on the root cause of acne and help reduce it.

Sweating

Personal hygiene is another important subject to discuss with both sexes before puberty, because as soon as puberty starts sweat glands under the arms and around the genitals roar into full production, pouring out sweat which, if your kids are not used to it, will lead to BO and a multitude of social problems at school. Most body-odour problems can be avoided by washing regularly and wearing clean clothes; however, boys need to pay special attention to cleaning under their foreskin and girls to keeping clean when their periods are on. As embarrassing as this is to talk about, it's an essential part of sex and relationships education, as having BO will affect how they feel about themselves and how others react to them. A simple explanation that they're going to smell if they don't wash regularly should have them rushing to the bathroom.

Feeling blue (mood swings)

Worry, anxiety and depressive thoughts – they happen to us all, but during puberty your kids may feel them so strongly that they'll just want to stay in bed and pull the sheets up over their heads. While these moods are natural and the result of the huge range of changes going on in the body, if your child becomes unresponsive and insular and/or radically changes his or her behaviour, seek advice from your GP. In the meantime be sure to keep talking about depression and low mood swings and what may trigger it. Areas to look at include:

- **Body image and self-esteem.** How does your child feel about his or her body? And what images are they looking at that may make them feel good/bad about themselves? Look at their magazines and DVDs, and watch the programmes they are watching for clues.
- **School life and friendships.** Has their friendship circle changed? Do you know what's going on at school apart from their grades and exams? Is your child lonely or under some sort of peer pressure? Use TV programmes and soap operas to trigger discussion.
- **Negative feelings your children may hold about themselves.** Does your child value himself/herself? Or do they feel not good enough in some way? Are they under too much stress to fit in or to pass exams? These are subjects that need to be discussed.

Weight problems

Prior to puberty your children may have been as thin as a piece of spaghetti, but with puberty comes weight gain and with it a multitude of potential problems that affect self-esteem, confidence and how we relate to the opposite sex. Never say 'diet' to your kids, but work on the healthy-food principle. Vegetables, fruit, brown bread, milk, fish and lean meats – get them willingly to fill their bodies with these foods and they'll be bursting with energy and will lose weight too.

- With weight loss the equation to get across is simple – eat good foods and you'll feel good. Eat fewer calories (the energy value of food) and expend more energy (through activity) and you'll lose weight. Eat food that screams variety and you'll fill your body with a range of vitamins and nutrients that will not only make you look good, but also feel stronger and fitter.

- If your children want to get healthy and lose weight, make them eat breakfast. According to the Office for National Statistics, one in five kids skips breakfast – that's 3 million kids each day. The reason behind the need for breakfast is simple: the body needs fuel in the morning because it hasn't eaten for at least ten hours. Deprive it of this and it will run on empty and then retaliate at 11am, at lunchtime and pretty much all day. Studies also show that skipping breakfast often leads people to eat more calories per day, as they opt for a larger lunch and more afternoon snacks.

- Get them active. Your children don't have to be sports stars to be fit. Government guidelines recommend that all under-eighteens do one hour of exercise every single day. It sounds daunting, but exercise is cumulative, meaning it can be spread in segments throughout the day. Either twenty minutes before school, twenty at lunchtime and twenty after school, or ten minutes scattered six times through the day. For instance:

TIME	GET FIT ACTIVITY
10 mins	Walk to school instead of taking the bus
10 mins	Walk with friends at lunchtime
20 mins	Walk home via the shops or the park
20 mins	Play football or dance around your room

Shyness and confidence problems

Not all children are born boisterous or get bolshy when they hit their teens. Many become introverted; girls especially see their self-esteem plummeting and with it their confidence. If you notice your child becoming introverted, here's how to help them overcome it:

- Talk about being defined by other people's labels. Also known as 'Challenge people's perspective of you'. Their teacher thinks they should speak up, their friends think they are sensible and you think they need a confidence boost – what do they think? Encourage your child to choose who they want to be and give them a sense of achievement about who they are.
- Discuss how shyness is learnt behaviour. While we're not all born extroverts, shyness does tend to be learnt, which is good news because it means your child can unlearn it. Help them work out what they are getting from being shy (remember, none of us ever does anything painful that doesn't give us a positive outcome). Does it help them feel safe? Does it give them an excuse to stop trying?
- Get them to think about how being shy affects their

behaviour. Does it put them at the mercy of friends with stronger wills? Or make them attracted to friends who are more confident? How would they stand up to peer pressure?

Problems with parents, teachers and friends

Growing up often means growing away from people, seeking independence and fighting authority. In other words, your child may turn into someone who has a bit of an attitude problem when it comes to adults. If you have talked honestly to your son or daughter throughout the whole of his or her life and have a good line of communication going, he or she should still talk to you. However, whereas once your child turned to you for help and advice, now the opinion of friends will take centre stage. To turn your kid into a competent adult who can manage his or her own life, there comes a time when you need to step back and let them take more control. This doesn't mean giving them total freedom, but letting them know you trust them to make the right decisions.

If your child has a sense of outrage about the way they are being treated, listen to what they are saying before dismissing their rants. Yes, the likelihood is they are making a mountain out of a molehill, but to them it is a mountain and they need your help to get over it. If you just keep saying 'no' to everything, or taking the other person's side, you will only increase their sense of outrage and the idea that you 'don't understand'. Listen, discuss and give a little (and never, ever say 'I told you so') and you will get credit for not only being flexible but approachable too.

YOUR QUESTIONS ANSWERED

Q I am worried about my thirteen-year-old daughter. Recently she came to me and told me that she was worried because all her friends have breasts and have started their periods while she is, as she said, 'still as flat as a pancake'. She also mentioned they all have boyfriends, so to make her feel better I said, 'Don't worry – you'll find someone soon', and instead she got really upset and accused me of not understanding her. Help!

A Your daughter isn't looking for reassurance that she'll get a boyfriend one day, but that her lack of periods and breasts is normal. It's very natural for girls to compare themselves to their peer group, and being a late developer has made her feel left behind and apart from her friends. Go back to her and tell her you've checked out the information regarding puberty and that it's 100 per cent normal not to have developed yet. If she's not reassured, ask her if she'd like to see the GP just to put her mind at rest. This way she'll see that you not only understand but are taking her worries seriously too.

Q I am a single mother of an eleven-year-old boy and I am desperate to talk to him about sex education, but whenever I start to tell him something he shouts, 'Don't, Mum' and puts his hands over his ears. It's partly my fault, because I've avoided the subject for so long that we're both now embarrassed by it. He doesn't have a dad on the scene so I'm not sure what to do.

A There are a number of ways to broach this. Try the open-notebook tactic: leave a notebook and pen in his bedroom and tell him if he has any questions he's too embarrassed to ask he can write them down and you'll answer them in the book. If that doesn't work, try being completely honest and ask him outright who he'd like to talk to about sex and relationships. Maybe there is an uncle, family friend or teacher with whom he feels more comfortable and whom you could ask to be his mentor. The sex basics aside, you can still talk to him about relationships, friendships and even his expectations about love. Use the programmes you watch together as a way to spark discussion and gently get him used to discussing and thinking about emotions and the nature of relationships with you.

Q My ten-year-old daughter lives with me and my girlfriend because she doesn't get on with her mum. We have a close and friendly father/daughter relationship (especially as her mum is in Spain) but even though she gets on with my girlfriend, they are not close. Because of this I know I have to be the one to start talking to her about sex and love, but it makes me nervous. My inclination is to scare her out of having sex, especially as she's already asking me questions about boys and kissing.

A The temptation for many fathers is to duck the issue, so it's a good sign that you're keen to give it a go and an even better sign that your daughter has an open relationship where she feels she can ask you things. As tempting as it is, the key is not to go in heavy handed, threatening all kinds of repercussions should she get into trouble or scaring her about boys. Do this and all that will happen is she'll hide what's going on. It's far better to answer her questions honestly and simply with statements such as, 'Well, I know boys try that because of X and Y, but remember, it's better always to do what feels right for you and not let them pressure you into it.' It also helps to talk to her about your own experience of growing up and be honest about feeling embarrassed. This way she'll know you're being genuine, and it will help set the stage for the more serious questions and topics that need to be discussed.

Q I am shocked at how much my nine-year-old seems to know about sex. The other day she came home from school and I heard her say 'erection' and 'wet dream' when she was teasing her eight-year-old brother. I told her off right away, which I now regret, but I was shocked. I suppose it's a sign to talk to her about sex, but have I left it too late?

A The chances are that although your daughter is throwing around terms like erection and wet dream, she has very little understanding of what they mean or how they relate to sex and relationships. What this incident means is that you need to start discussing puberty, relationships and sex with her so she doesn't end up with a warped idea of what sex is. She may already have got the idea from you that sex isn't spoken about in your house, so you may have to start by apologizing for telling her off and asking her where she heard those words and what she thinks they mean. Try to keep things light hearted and casual when you do this so she doesn't think she's in more trouble and clam up. Then explain what they do mean in simple terms. For example: 'An erection is when a boy's penis gets hard'; 'A wet dream is when boys get excited and think they have wet the bed.' And use her response as a way of seeing where she is in the sex and relationships stakes.

4

SEX, LOVE AND RELATIONSHIPS

TRUE LOVE – COME ON, BE HONEST, WE ALL WANT IT. WE ALL want that someone special to cuddle up to, to feel close to and to love us when we're bad-tempered, whether we're fourteen or forty years old. We also all want to be with someone who makes our heart melt, our knees wobble and then looks at us and wants to have passionate sex. Though when it's your kids that we're talking about, you're probably hoping that last bit happens when they are at least twenty-five with a flat and income of their own. The trouble is, even if that is the case (and it happens), it doesn't stop them wanting love right now, yearning for it and even seeking it out!

Like anyone who has had a relationship, I'm the first to admit I've made mistakes and poor decisions, many of them when I was young and vulnerable. Like loads of teenagers, I suffered from low self-esteem and as a result went out with guys who asked me, not because I liked them (I didn't even think about that) but more because I was so grateful they liked me. And that's the problem with being inexperienced and not understanding either yourself or what makes relationships tick: it leads to bad choices and to doing things just to make people love you or because you think that's how love is supposed to work. Take the girls who stay in violent relationships because they believe love can change someone, or the girls who have sex too early because their friends are doing it or because they don't know how to say no in case they lose someone they love. Avoid telling your children about what makes a healthy relationship and what doesn't, or how peer pressure operates, and they'll have a lopsided approach to love. And this is the big flaw in the way many of our schools teach sex and relationship education. It doesn't take a genius to see that the biological gets emphasized because it's compulsory and the relationship stuff is brushed aside because it's not. This would be fine if we were a 'talky' nation like, say, Holland, and couldn't wait to explore our inner feelings with each other – but we're not, which means for most young people the relationship side of life is a complicated maze that they often have to battle through on their own.

Some young people are lucky. Stephanie, aged fifteen, is engaged to her boyfriend Danny. She respects her mum and knows it's mutual. 'If I listen to her she will listen to me,' says Stephanie. 'Since I was little she has always told me anything I needed to know. You know when older kids say things in the playground – I would go home and tell my mum and she would sit down and tell me. At school they teach you about biological terms and things, and it's all well and good having the facts, but when you get in that situation it's hard to know what to do. They don't tell you about emotions and how you're going to feel and what you will be thinking – my mum told me that.'

If you want your kids to have a healthy attitude to relationships, fall in love happily and avoid as much heartbreak (and bad dates) as possible, teach them how to do it. This means talking about the good as well as the bad so that (a) they know the difference between a good and a bad relationship; (b) they have high expectations of falling in love; and (c) they can use this information to suss out when they're being taken for a ride.

LOVE AND RELATIONSHIPS

Is it in the stars? Is it random chance, fate or luck that makes us fall in love? Well, how we love and with whom we choose to fall in love is a lot less romantic and has much to do with what we witness and experience. For your children this means that much of what they believe about love and relationships relates back to how you, their parents, act, communicate and get on, as well as the films they watch, the books they read and what their friends tell them. Observing you work through your relationship is one of the most important elements of relationship education, as it will form the foundations of their beliefs about how people in love negotiate and behave. If you're thinking, 'Oh my God!', relax: thankfully this doesn't mean you have to be on best behaviour all the time, as the aim is to give them a realistic view of relationships rather than a sugar-coated one. It does, however, mean that you need to talk about the relationship stuff as much as the sex stuff, so that they aren't confused by mixed messages or see one thing and translate it as another.

Have your kids, for instance, grown up seeing you close and happy or have they watched you criticizing each other? Perhaps you live in a home where everyone is very polite and never says what is on their mind – or is everything OTT and dramatic? Have you unwittingly been showing your kids that love and relationships are a destructive thing? To help your children unravel the information they've picked up, talk about some of the following with them. Again, relationships and love are huge subjects that can't be covered in one blast, so pick and mix your topics and broach things that you feel are relevant to your kids and what they're going through.

- Talk about the good stuff. Tell them what you've got out of being in love – mention friendship, humour, good times and pleasure, alongside physical attraction. Mention examples of good relationships and couples who work in sync, then ask your teenagers to describe their ideal relationship and see how close or how far apart your views are.
- Show them how to resolve differences within a relationship. This is a great way to get your young people to realize that relationships have ups and downs and take negotiation to get right. Ask them to tell you how they think people should behave if they disagree. Whether you can disagree and still be in love? And finally, how big decisions should be made in a relationship.
- Watch what they're watching. Soaps, magazines, books and even music all give a very different view of relationships and love, and in the same way that media can

affect attitudes to sex, they can also build expectations about relationships. To find out what your children are learning from their viewing, try making comments about the relationships and actions of couples on TV. For example: 'Do you think X should have done that to Y? Do you think he loves her if he can do that to her?'

- Don't forget very young kids. Talking to under-eights about love and relationships may seem a bit ridiculous, but you can still discuss much of the above (and again start building a base to lay other information on as they get older) in terms of communication and negotiation by using examples of their behaviour and actions with siblings and friends, as well as with you.

'What do I wish I'd known? I wish I'd known how to talk to girls. I hadn't the faintest idea. I thought they were from another planet. Somebody should have told me how girls think and what they're like. I was hugely unsuccessful in the early years in forming any kind of relationship because I thought girls just thought like boys and I had no idea of their gentle nature and need for affection and affirmation.'

DR COLM O'MAHONY

Love's ups and downs

The problem with love is, when it happens we all tend to be ruled by our hearts, not our heads! We make choices that feel good and give instant gratification, rather than doing what's logical and sensible. This doesn't mean that all your good work on relationships will go to waste, but rather that your kids need to learn by their mistakes the way we did. The biggest problem is that many young people view relationships and falling in love idealistically, not only expecting their relationships to be filled with joy, but assuming that when they love someone they need to prove it. These assumptions can lead to all kinds of problems, especially when sex comes into the frame. Here are some ways to help your son or daughter handle relationship pressure.

Give them ways to stand up for themselves

It's vital to talk about manipulation and coercion – and not just from a loved one but from friends as well. Sixteen-year-old Kerry pointed out that sex is a double-edged sword for most kids: 'You get people saying if a girl has slept with someone she is a slag, but then you get other people saying, "Little Miss Virgin over there", and so some people can end up feeling like, "Oh, everyone is having sex but me", and not know what to do or say.'

One good way to help teenagers is to make suggestions or give them phrases to help them slip out of pressurized situations. For instance:

- If they are being asked to do something they don't feel is right for them, suggest they say: 'I'm not into this – let's talk about it.' The aim is to make it 100 per cent clear that they don't like what they are being asked to do, but that for the sake of the relationship they are willing to discuss why.
- If they are being pressurized into sex with the words 'You would if you loved me', get them to respond with

'You wouldn't push me if you loved me.' The aim here is to get them to see that people who really love them will not make them do things they don't want to do.

- When facing a cheating partner or one that doesn't treat them right – ask them if they would treat someone they care about this way?

Talk about what love can and can't give them

Let's be honest – we all have expectations about love and your children will start to formulate theirs from an early age. This is why it's important to discuss what love can give them and what it won't give them, and to emphasize that, although love with the right person can bring happiness, joy, a sense of direction and pleasure, it won't make anyone happy if they're not happy already. Looking for fulfilment through someone else has to be talked about, as it can lead to disappointment and regrets. Also be aware that not having a boyfriend/girlfriend can be a lonely place for a teenager and can lead young people to feel as if there is something wrong with them because no-one wants them.

The problem with this kind of thinking is that it can become self-destructive: teenagers can easily start feeling 'not good enough' and start believing, 'If only I was thinner/stronger/taller/prettier I'd have someone.' So while it's important to discuss relationships, it's also essential to emphasize that having one isn't everything and not having one definitely isn't a sign of being a loser. Look for examples around you to support this and at the same time encourage your son or daughter to go after other things besides a boyfriend/girlfriend.

Talk about the bad stuff

While most relationships have their ups and downs, there are signs when a relationship is unhealthy and it's worth knowing them and passing them on to your kids, because if they are in a bad relationship you, like them, may be the last to know. Get your children to consider what they are willing to accept and not accept in the name of love (use examples real or otherwise to get them to see the repercussions of a bad relationship). Also help them to see that any incidence of abuse in a relationship, whether it's verbal (the way someone speaks to you and says things to you), physical (pushing, slapping, kicking, punching and biting) or mental (manipulation and bullying), is a predictor of more serious problems to come.

Signs of a bad relationship that you should look out for:

- Your child is often apologetic about the behaviour of his/her partner; she/he either hides the bad stuff from you, makes excuses for them, or claims that he/she's OK on the inside.
- Your teenager's partner makes all the decisions in the relationship, controls your child's behaviour, and checks up on his/her whereabouts.
- The partner is extremely jealous and insults, humiliates or puts your son or daughter down in front of others.
- Your teenager has unexplained injuries and the explanations he/she offers don't make sense.
- Your child starts talking about herself/himself in a very negative way and stops seeing friends.

Give your child the tools to get out of an abusive relationship by letting them know support is always available at home and teaching them where to go outside of the home if they feel desperate for some objective advice and information (see Resources).

Mention self-esteem again

I know I've banged on about self-esteem before, but it really is worth talking about again, because if your kids have good reserves of self-esteem and value themselves, they won't rely on others to do it – meaning they'll be less likely to jump into bed for the wrong reasons. Kerry-Ann, for instance, talked openly about her own teenage mistakes so that her daughter would value her worth. 'I was so clingy when I lost mine and wanted to be loved. Stephanie knows she's loved and she knows she doesn't need to have sex to feel loved.'

To help your kids keep their self-esteem high, make sure they know what they're worth by:

- Praising their behaviour (we do this with young kids all the time but forget about the older ones).
- Helping them to see their talents (social, academic, sporting, etc.).
- Boosting their confidence in their decisions – literally by telling them they did the right thing.
- Getting them to make their own value judgements about situations – don't tell them what to think, let them decide.

Help them manage their emotions

There's no denying it: puberty, falling in love and starting up a relationship is a stressful time and often it's made harder by the struggle to come to terms with weird new emotions (feeling weak at the knees in someone's presence, for instance) and intense feelings like needing someone really badly. Telling your child they are too young to be in love doesn't make it any less intense for them. They are feeling love and need you to listen and hear this, and allow them both to express it and to feel it.

To help them boost their relationship skills it's worth discussing that, while certain emotions are easy to deal with, others – such as anger, frustration and irritation – take time to manage, especially when you're supposed to be happily in love. The trick is to get your kids to gain a greater understanding of their emotions before they fall in love. For instance, use their own moods to get them to think about what makes them feel the way they do:

- **Get them to highlight their triggers.** Does being told what to do or being teased make them angry and aggressive? Does being talked over and not listened to make them frustrated? Help them to recognize their triggers and make the root of anger clear to people.
- **What makes them feel better?** What makes them feel listened to – an understanding of what went wrong or the other person saying 'I'm sorry'? It's important to add here that they may not get what they are looking for, so you need to help them find ways to manage their emotions even when they don't. For instance, they might

try counting to ten and taking (literal) time out if they have a short temper; or using a diary or sport to help vent their frustrations; and talking to you if they feel stuck and furious.

- **How they may antagonize others.** This is a hard one to discuss because it involves making your teenager take a critical look at himself/herself. If you have a good relationship, constructive criticism may go down well here (small tip – if you're currently in a place where nothing you say is right, don't go here). A better way to approach it is to ask your child what he/she feels are bad points and weak areas. By highlighting what they feel they need to work on, you can help your child manage his/her emotions.

SEX AND RELATIONSHIPS

At some point your child's raging hormones are going to connect with someone else's, and physical attraction will hit big time. While your first reaction may be abject horror that the issue of having sex is nigh already, do bear in mind that, while the timing of that momentous event may be out of your hands, talking about sex in regard to love will help delay it.

The first thing to talk about is lust versus love. As adults we all know that feeling: you spot someone across the room and suddenly your stomach flips and you think you're in the grip of love at first sight. Experience helps us to recognize that it's more likely to be lust at first sight fuelled by our hormones, but when it happens for the first time ever it can be hard to distinguish. This is why it pays to highlight and expound the virtues of the getting-to-know-each-other part of relationships.

HOW TO HELP WITH RELATIONSHIP ANGST

❈ **Don't rush to give advice**

Often this is not what your kids will be looking for: mostly they just want to be understood, not have you try to fix all their worries. If you keep jumping in they'll just assume you haven't heard what they have said.

❈ **Don't dismiss the problem**

Even if a problem seems small and inconsequential to you, it's a major concern for them. Also saying, 'Oh that's normal, you'll get over it,' translates as 'I'm not interested in helping you.' It gives the message that you don't understand or are not willing to listen.

❈ **Offer reassurance, encouragement and support**

Provide stability and predictability, and encourage them to participate in family life.

❈ **Talk about how you deal with problems**

Emphasize problem-solving skills by getting them to think round their difficulty. For example, how can I change my response to this problem and make myself feel better, instead of how can I change X's response.

❈ **Teach them safe ways to take time out from their problems**

Music, TV and sport all help here, as does talking to friends and family.

This might sound impossible, but it can be done, and without the aid of superhuman powers.

Of course, in the heady world of teenage love, where a month often constitutes a long-term relationship, this getting-to-know-each-other stuff can sound tediously dull, but it is a tactic that works.

The next area to highlight is: does love equal sex and does sex equal love? This is also one of the major pitfalls of first love – the assumption that all couples who love each other have to have sex to prove it, or that having sex automatically leads to love. As we know, it's not true, but teenagers need to get their heads round this by realizing that sexual intercourse is just a physical act, not one that triggers attachment or emotions that aren't there already.

Likewise, being in love doesn't mean you have to engage in sex to feel grown up, or to prove to yourself or prove to your partner – or even prove to your friends – that you've got the real thing going. Try to get your kids to see that, while it's easy to have sex, it's definitely not easy to live with the consequences, especially if you've done it for the wrong reasons. Below are some other issues worth talking about.

The pressure to have sex

'If you really loved me you'd have sex' is one of the most common ways one person tries to coerce another into sex. It works by playing on the idea that you need to show/prove your love because the other person is saying they don't believe you love them as much as they love you. In reality they are trapping you with a no-win statement. Either you prove you love them by having sex or you say no, which then 'proves' that you don't love them. It's sneaky and manipulative and more common than you might think. If your teenager can't see the emotional blackmail behind this sentence, say, 'If you really loved me you would stay at home with me every night until you are thirty years old.' Trust me, they're likely to see the ridiculousness of this statement right away (and if not, you may have company on the sofa for another fifteen years).

How to say no and mean it

How assertive are your teenagers in the real world? They may have no problem getting their voice heard at home, but with friends and at school can they communicate their feelings easily or are they too afraid to stand their ground? Watch them with their friends and listen to how they negotiate their friendships. If this is not a strong area for them, teach them how to be assertive.

Again it pays to start young. Even very young children of three or four can be taught to shout 'Stop!' as a keep-away sign to siblings invading their space and/or other children trying to take their toys. This is the same technique to use with your teenagers – albeit with different words and under different circumstances. The aim is to get your kids to learn to say no to manipulation and peer pressure *with authority*, so point out that it's no good them saying no to sex if they remain half dressed and cuddled up to the person asking. Likewise, if someone's hand travels somewhere they don't want it to be while kissing, saying no and then carrying on kissing gives out a mixed message.

How to express love without sex

Helping young people to see that it's more than possible to express love without sex is another handy tool to give them. One way to make them see this is to get them thinking about how they show their love to friends and family members. Obviously they'll twig this kind of love is a bit different, but the aim is to point out that love can be expressed in many ways in any relationship – through words, gestures, respect, body language, consideration, and just being there for someone.

If you then ask them how they think love can be proved, you'll get an idea of where they are in their relationship. If they say gifts, or by doing what someone wants, you'll know that they need more relationship confidence and a better understanding of how to show someone you love them.

It also hints that maybe they have a partner who is pressurizing them, though this isn't always the case, as some people do just go into relationships believing they have constantly to prove their love with gestures. This is usually a sign of low self-esteem and shows you need to help them see they are worthy of someone's love by again talking about good personality traits, social skills and what they think they have to offer someone (this will give you an idea of what areas to focus on).

Not everyone is doing it

Statistics show that, contrary to popular belief, we don't live in a country where all our teenagers are busy romping every night. Most people in fact wait until they are sixteen or over, but it's still worth discussing this point with your kids because one of the areas that may hit them is peer pressure from friends. It's no good just saying 'Be an individual', because the need to fit in and be just like your mates is huge when you're young. And there's no point in coming out with the old classic, 'If they jumped off a cliff would you follow them?' because the answer is 'Yes'.

It takes great strength to stand up for what you believe in if it means standing away from your friends – but it can be done. First, you need to talk about whether a real friend would pressurize you to do something that you obviously don't want to do. Again, use examples from family life or from television scenarios. Second, talk about the issue of privacy. Point out that, while it's nice to share your emotional ups and downs with friends, your sex life is personal: you don't (and for the sake of your relationship shouldn't) tell them when you have sex, if you're having sex or whether you've decided against sex.

How to keep their wits about them

People who pressurize their partners into sex are smart. They pick their moments wisely and tend to choose times when they know their partner is more vulnerable to their words, so it pays to get your kids to look after themselves. Alcohol and drugs in particular will work against them, as these will lower their inhibitions and weaken their judgement. While this fact is obvious, many young people, especially the shy ones, think of alcohol and drugs as confidence boosters and something to help them loosen up. Getting your kids to be drink/drug wise is as important as all the above relationship skills because being under their influence is the one thing that will lead them to be taken advantage of. The way to ensure your children are smart about drink and drugs is to educate them in the same way you are educating them about sex and relationships. Give them information so they can make informed decisions and not be led astray by a 'friend' who encourages them to experiment (see Resources for drink and drugs information).

How to be sure they're ready

Can you remember how you knew you were ready for sex? Was it a practical decision or one made because you got carried away? Were you in love or in lust? Infatuated or intoxicated? Did you regret it or love it? The chances are that, whatever your reasons, you were in a bit of a dilemma about it, which is where your kids will be prior to going for it.

> 'I regret having sex at twelve with someone who didn't matter to me – I really regret that. I wouldn't just sleep with anyone now because I totally disagree with that after what happened to me. But I do think sex is different for boys and girls. Girls, when they are younger they have all these fairy tales, "Oh, I'll wait till I'm married and to the right person." But for boys they like to see who can lose their virginity first. My advice to all the girls out there is: wait till you are ready and have found the right person. Don't do it because your mates are doing it.'
>
> KERRY, 16

Questions that determine if they are ready:

- Are they under peer pressure – are their friends egging them on?
- Are they doing it to fit in – because they don't want to be different?
- Are they in a relationship?
- Do they have a gut feeling that it's right for them?
- Is it a need for excitement – because they're bored?

Virginity and the age of consent

According to the Sexual Offences Act 2003 it is a criminal offence for any kind of sexual activity to take place between two people where one or both participants is under sixteen. The law applies to men and women, whether gay, lesbian or straight in England, Wales and Scotland. In Northern Ireland, the same law applies except the age of consent is seventeen. The law is designed to protect anyone who is under sixteen from abuse by adults, and while it's rare that it's used to prosecute consensual teenage sexual behaviour, be aware that boys can still be prosecuted if they indulge in sexual activity and/or have sex with a girl who is under sixteen.

The problem with the age of consent is that many teenagers see it as a guide to when to have sex. While it can be a useful tool in getting kids to delay sex, it's essential that they don't then think they have to have sex once they reach sixteen. Take eighteen-year-old Femi, who, having lost his virginity at sixteen, now believes this isn't the right age to have sex: 'Seventeen or eighteen is better because you've just come out of school and you actually know what you're doing more. People have sex at sixteen because, when I was at school, there was pressure to lose your virginity. I want others to know it doesn't matter if you lose your virginity at twenty – it's no big deal.'

Virginity is also worth discussing, as there's a double standard pervading this area: nice girls don't have sex, and real men do! Virginity is sold to boys as something to be ashamed about and something to lose as quickly as possible, spurred on by exaggerated stories from their mates and/or pressure from girlfriends to 'be a man'. For girls, meanwhile, virginity is often seen as something to hold on to and something that gives them extra kudos and reward in the love stakes. Both versions are wrong, just adding extra pressure and guilt to kids about what having sex really means.

A WORD ABOUT SEXUALITY

If you don't know anyone who is gay, the chances are the only time the subject of sexuality comes up is if you watch it on TV or if someone in your house makes a joke about it. The problem with being gay is not actually being gay, but the strong and prejudiced notions people hold about it. Contrary to certain opinion, people don't choose to be gay, in the same way others don't choose to be heterosexual – it's the way we are born and there's not a lot we can do about it. However, there is a lot you can do to reassure your kids about their sexuality (whatever it is) and to improve their attitude to homosexuality as a whole. You may think, 'Why bother?' Well for starters, if your child is gay or worried about some same-sex feelings he/she may be having (which doesn't necessarily indicate they are gay), making the subject a no-go area in your house will just send the message that it's both wrong and something to be feared. That aside, at some point in their life your kids are going to go out into the world and meet people who are gay so, unless you want them to have a bigoted fear of gay people, it pays to talk about sexuality with them.

Accepting differences

As adults we are able to handle diversity as well as to appreciate how it can widen our world, but when you're a teenager, so busy trying to fit in and be like everyone else, you can lose sight of the fact that it's OK to be different. This is why it's important to talk about sexuality, emphasizing that while you don't have to like or even agree with how another person lives, it's illogical to hate them for it. Many teenagers (boys in particular) react strongly to the idea of homosexuality, mostly due to fear of the unknown and a warped idea of what it is. This is why you need to dispel myths – for instance, people don't choose to be gay and being gay doesn't mean you fancy every person of the same sex. Speak positively about homosexuality as early as possible, so that your children grow up knowing it's just another way of being, rather than something menacing and scary. Ways to do this are simply to talk about differences and avoid creating myths yourself by generalizing about gay people.

Same-sex crushes

During puberty many kids have a same-sex crush, when they suddenly feel drawn to someone they know or are close to already. Usually (but not always) this is fuelled by admiration of some sort, so if your teenager is confiding in you over this, try not to overreact and either label them or tell them they're being silly. While some people are certain of their sexuality from an early age, others experience teenage same-sex crushes only to go on to realize they are straight. Give your child time to come to terms with whatever sexual orientation feels right for them. Their decision may not be what you want, but if you want them to grow up with a strong sense of self, you sometimes have to swallow your own feelings and learn to accept who your child is.

Coming out

If your child knows he/she is gay, at some point you will want them to tell you (you might be thinking 'No way', but do you really want your son or daughter to live a lie for your benefit?). Whether they do this or not depends mainly on how you've discussed sexuality within your home, your expectations for their future and how comfortable they feel about being honest with you. Keep sexuality an open subject and your kids will feel confident about telling you who they are rather than feeling forced to live two different lives. If you feel shocked and upset this is normal, but try to remember that your child is the same person he/she was before telling you. Nothing has changed but your perception of them. If they can see you're upset you need to explain why. Is it fear for their future? Dismay that they may not be going down the marriage-and-two-kids path? Or simply worry that life may not be easy for them? Finally, if your child has come out to you or hints that he/she is gay, remember you haven't made them gay but you should be pleased that your approach to sex and relationship education has given them the courage to be 100 per cent honest and open with you.

YOUR KIDS' PRE-SEX WORRIES

Your only worry may be that they have sex before you think they're ready, but if your kids are in love and about to lose their L-plates then they're going to have other worries lurking just below the surface. Of course, one tactic is to ignore their fears and hope it keeps them from having sex, but sadly I have to tell you that this doesn't work. All that will happen is they'll have sex and feel bad about themselves. Think back and you may recall that the things no-one ever tells you about sex are:

- It takes time to get right.
- It can be embarrassing.
- It can hurt.
- It takes time to be good at it.
- Boys don't know any more or less than girls.
- Girls aren't more honest than boys.
- Having more partners doesn't make you better at it.

So if you suspect your kids are feeling worried, inhibited and afraid of having sex, let them work their way through the following.

THE OTHER SIDE OF THE COIN
Pre-Sex Worries

The time will come when you're in love and think that you may be ready to have sex. But, as certain and excited as you may feel, you are probably also a bit worried – perhaps even a little bit afraid. The fact is, it's normal to feel apprehensive – most people do. Here are some of the most common worries and how to deal with them.

Worry: You believe you look horrible naked

Having sex involves getting naked and that's part of the fun of it, but if you're not comfortable in your birthday suit then you're not going to be comfortable having sex. Why? Well, because if you are overly self-conscious you're going to spend more time sucking in your stomach and clenching your bum than enjoying what's going on. To feel better naked and improve the way you feel about your body, get used to seeing yourself without clothes. Don't worry – I am not suggesting you turn your home into a nudist colony (and freak your parents out) but simply get used to seeing your naked reflection in a full-length mirror. Once a day take a long, hard look and instead of focusing on what you hate, see your body as a complete image with good bits – because this is the way some-one else will look at you. Do it regularly and you'll desensitize yourself, build body confidence and stop worrying.

Worry: You believe that sex is dirty or bad

The truth is, your upbringing can squash your enjoyment of sex, especially if you grew up in a family that believed sex outside marriage was 'bad' or 'wrong' due to religious or cultural beliefs. If this rings true for you it may be worth considering the fact that sex – as long as it's between two consenting adults – is as natural and as normal as breathing. Talk if you can to your parents about their own feelings on sex and sex outside marriage. They may never agree that sex is a good thing for you, but at least you'll know where your feelings are coming from and so will be able to decide if they are right for you or not.

Worry: You believe that men like sex more than women

This is something that some men would have women believe and is usually the result of how they were brought up and/or who they spend their spare time with. No-one should feel guilty about their desire to have sex or about their sexual feelings, as they are totally normal and driven by biological as well as emotional impulses. Men don't want sex or need sex more than women: it's simply that they are allowed to express their desire more than women are (yes, double standards again!). If you have siblings of a different gender, listen to how they talk about sex or how your parents discuss sex with them. Is it different? Are the men in your house allowed to ogle women, while the women are 'encouraged' to remain demure?

'Girls who have one-night stands, it's the same as guys. If we can do it, they shouldn't be called sluts or anything.'

STEVEN, 18

Worry: You believe that men aren't made to be faithful

This is a popular myth that's thrown about by men who usually want an excuse for being unfaithful. The reality is that some men can't be faithful – but then neither can some women. This has little to do with 'biology' and more to do with their psychological make-up – i.e. how they view relationships and love. Some people cheat because they can't bear intimacy or because they like to sabotage the good things they have. Other people cheat because they literally can't keep it in their pants, and others still because they just don't think about what they're doing. If you don't believe men can be faithful then you need to examine where your beliefs are coming from. If you're simply worried that the person you're with will cheat, this is a definite sign that you're not ready to have sex with them, because you don't trust them.

'I think lasses get a bit more reserved because they get judged more than lads do. When I'm with the rest of the lads the first thing we talk about is "Have you knobbed anyone lately?" It's always who's done what. Lasses are different. They'll just tell one or two friends. If I heard lasses bragging about it I'd think they were sluts, but with us you're a stud if you brag about it more.'

RORY, 18

Worry: You believe that you won't be able to satisfy your partner

The number-one worry for most men is feeling they are not big enough and that size is an issue for women. In fact, you can relax – the female vagina is only 12.5 centimetres long and only the first 5 centimetres are sensitive, so even the smallest penis can do its job properly. The number-one fear for women is that they'll get it wrong. If that's your fear you can also relax, because there is no right or wrong way to have sex. Real sex, as opposed to cinematic sex, is sometimes embarrassing, noisy, laughable and awkward – and it really doesn't matter, because it's about being together, not about perfecting the art!

Worry: You're afraid sex will hurt

Sex does tend to hurt a bit the first time, usually because you're tense and anxious. When this happens it causes the muscles in the vagina to tense up and penetration becomes difficult and in some cases you won't be able to do it. This is perfectly normal and nothing to worry about. It usually means you need to slow down, have more foreplay and delay penetrative sex until your body is more lubricated and ready.

Worry: You're afraid of an unplanned pregnancy or a sexually transmitted infection (STI)

This is a fear that shouldn't be here if you have talked about contraception together and gone and sorted it out (see

Chapter 5 for more on this). Boys shouldn't just leave it to girls, and girls shouldn't let boys make the decision about whether to use something or not. To combat an unplanned pregnancy and an STI, always go Double Dutch – that's wear a condom and use the pill. You may think this is excessive, but the pill, if used properly, has a 98 per cent chance of stopping you getting pregnant and a condom will stop 98 per cent of all STIs (a condom can also prevent pregnancy, but it's not as good as the pill and isn't that easy to use if you're new to sex). If a partner is refusing to use contraception, see it as a loud alarm bell warning you that you're about to make a mistake. Anyone who cares about you (and themselves) will want to use protection.

YOUR QUESTIONS ANSWERED

Q My daughter is confused about what intimacy means. She is dating a boy who wants her to have sex and has told her that to be really close to him they have to have sex. How do I explain that this is the last way she'll feel close to him without getting angry and telling her this guy is using her?

A You need to explain that intimacy in a relationship is not about getting naked between the sheets but is about trust between partners. Feeling close occurs when two people can be themselves completely and share their deepest thoughts, feelings and emotions without being afraid that their partner will laugh or judge them or not love them any more. Physical intimacy – i.e. sex – usually comes after the above, and it means sharing your body openly, with trust that the other person will respect you. The problem here, as you can clearly see, is that your daughter's boyfriend is manipulating her into feeling she has to do something to feel closer to him. Talk to her about coercion and feeling pressurized into having sex, and give her useful tactics to explain to her boyfriend why sex won't be on the agenda for quite a while yet.

Q We've always spoken about sex openly in our house right from when our two boys were young. Now my fourteen-year-old son has come to me and said he is going to have sex with his girlfriend (also fourteen) and I am horrified. I thought the whole point of being open was to get him to delay sex and instead he's jumping into bed with someone without even thinking. I want to tell him he can't do it and shout a bit, but know I can't. I feel upset and am 100 per cent sure he's going to regret it. What do I do?

A While he may be thinking about having sex, he's come to you to talk about it before doing it – which shows he isn't just jumping into bed with any old girl, but wanting first to discuss the issue openly with you. This is a direct result of your being open with him, and it is your chance to cement what's been said by offering him advice and playing devil's advocate. Saying 'no' isn't going to work and will just stop all communication between the two of you, so sit down with him and find out why he thinks he's ready. Ask him what he feels about his current relationship, what his expectations are about sex and what he's decided to do about contraception. Also point out that he could be prosecuted for having sex with a minor. Remember, we can't always make our kids do things our way for ever; at some point we have to step back and hope that all the information we've given them is enough to help them make the right decision.

Q I am a divorced mother of a fifteen-year-old girl and a thirteen-year-old boy. I do talk to my children about sex education issues, but what really worries me is not the sex stuff but my daughter's relationship behaviour. She has a very callous attitude to her boyfriends and is often unfaithful to them (though isn't having sex yet) and treats them quite nastily. She's not a bad person, but she does always seem angry and takes it out on them – I often have to take calls from upset boys. When I try to tell her she should be nicer she claims I don't understand what it's like, but I do because I myself went through a very bad divorce seven years ago. How can I help her?

A Your situation highlights why relationship education is just as important as the sex bit. You need to talk to your daughter about her beliefs regarding men and relationships. Ask her what she means by 'You don't understand what it's like.' Is she being pressurized, treated badly herself or does she simply not know how to relate to men? You say you yourself had a bad divorce – that could well be the root of the problem. We all pick up messages about relationships and love from our parents, and she may have unresolved issues about her dad and what happened seven years ago. Ask her how she feels about this. Take the emphasis off telling her how to behave, start talking about relationship stuff and you'll be surprised at what she might tell you.

Q My husband and I are trying to educate our son and daughter about sex and relationships but the one problem is, no matter what we say, my son, who is twelve years old, comes out with horrible stuff about girls being, as he says, 'slags' and boys being men. It makes me so mad and I know it's coming from his friends. I don't want him to grow up with double standards and treat girls badly. How do I combat what he's getting from his friends?

A Never underestimate the power teenage boys have over each other to act stupidly and say the same stupid things. Right now his friends probably feel like the most important people in his life, so what he's doing is replicating their behaviour to fit in. Thankfully it won't always be this way, especially if you and your husband counteract everything he says with something that gets him thinking, and with firm boundaries about what's acceptable at home. For instance, the next time he calls a woman/girl a 'slag' – ask him if he thinks that you and his sister are 'slags' too? That should shock him into considering what he's saying. At the same time, talk to him about how standing up for what he believes in is a bigger sign of being a man than agreeing with his mates.

5

LOSING IT AND DOING IT

YES, THE MOMENT'S HERE: TIME TO ACTUALLY GET DOWN TO the basics and face the fact that your kids will be losing their virginity and having sex. You may have filled them in on the biology, got their heads round what love is (and what it isn't) and even taught them how to exorcise their inner demons, but here is where it all comes together. And you can rest assured that it really does come together in a good way if you've put in the groundwork.

Of course, as a parent I understand only too well how excruciating it's going to be to go from theoretical conversations such as 'One day when you have sex' to hearing your child say, 'I'm thinking about having sex', but what I've realized is that if your son or daughter comes to you with those words you're actually a lucky parent, because it means your child trusts you. So my first bit of advice in this area is try not to be shocked by what your children tell you. I know it's almost impossible, but you've got to try to bite the bullet and hear what they're saying about sex and feeling ready. Second, as tempting as it is, don't just say 'No you're not' and then lock them in the cellar until they're thirty. From talking to the kids on this programme I can see now that this is just a naïve response. Your children have come to you because they feel they are ready, which means at this point it's too late to tell them to wait.

RESPECTING TEENAGERS' PRIVACY

Let's be honest: even if you have spent years preparing your kids and talking to them openly about sex and relationships, there are certain things they will not want to discuss with you, such as the logistics of the event or the finer points of what to do. They may tell you they are thinking about having sex, or are having sex, or want to have sex, but try to discuss either the actual sex bit with them or their worries about having sex and they'll run for the hills. The reality is, your children want to keep some things private in the same way that you probably still hide your sex life from your own parents. Respect their need for privacy by not prying too hard or asking too many questions and they'll still come to you with their problems and for help. As a result, you won't have to worry about them doing something high risk or self-destructive, nor fear they are crying alone in a corner somewhere.

Also, just a word about your children having sex. You may not want them to do it, and you may be angry if they do, but be aware that if they're hell bent on it and feel they are ready, they will have sex anyway and once they do they'll need you just as much as ever. Sex and relationship education doesn't just stop when sex happens; in fact it's needed even more after that point because, let's face it, sex can be scary. It can be intense and nerve-racking and full of unrealistic expectations. So there are two ways to look at this chapter – either read it and leave it open somewhere for your kids to peruse at their leisure, or broach it with them and gauge from their reaction whether they want to discuss it further with you or not. For this reason it's written directly to teenagers.

THE OTHER SIDE OF THE COIN
Moving Towards a Sexual Relationship

'How do you know when you're ready for sex? That's difficult, because everybody is different. Obviously, I don't think intercourse early on in a relationship is a great start. I think love and affection are important and the sexual contact can build up, through heavy petting, for example, until it becomes obvious that both parties want it without coercion.'

DR COLM O'MAHONY

Knowing you're ready

Knowing you're ready is a mixed bag for most people and is usually determined by where they are in a relationship, how far they have already gone in terms of sexual activity and what they hope sex will bring to the relationship. Aspects of a relationship that may equal being ready to have sex:

- You have a solid relationship based on trust. This means you love each other, like each other and know that you can trust each other because you already confide in each other and have discussed wanting to have sex.
- You have had a conversation regarding contraception and safer sex. You've talked about ensuring you are both protected from an unplanned pregnancy and sexually

transmitted infections and have decided what contraception is best for you. You also know where to go to get it and how it works.

- You have a relationship that's already intimate and close. You have already started moving towards sex in your relationship by going beyond kissing and both feel as if you want to and are ready to take it further.

Sexual expectations

Visions of the first time – a romantic soft-focus delight with orgasms all round. Mmm … think clumsy, relatively fast and messy, because that's a bit closer to the truth. You may believe sex is going to be the most fantastic thing in the world, and while the first time can be enjoyable, good sex between two people is a learnt and practised thing, the result of getting to know each other mentally and physically. So if you think you're both ready, here are some questions to discuss together:

- What contraception are you going to use?
- What do you think sex is going to be like? (If you find this question so excruciatingly embarrassing you can't ask it, should you really be getting naked with this person?)
- What's going to happen post-sex?
- What do you believe sex will do to your relationship?

Arousal and masturbation

Sexual urges, sexual fantasies and a need to get closer to someone you're dating are just a few signs that you could be heading towards sex. The first thing to do is regard these urges as normal. You're not weird or abnormal because you look at something and get aroused, or kiss someone you fancy and feel yourself getting excited. One area that you might decide to explore is masturbation – where you literally rub your genitals either to feel good or to bring on an orgasm. Masturbation causes a lot of shock and horror amongst most people, but it's normal and even younger children do it because they know it feels nice. (Note to parents: freak out about your kids masturbating and they are more likely to find other ways to release their sexual tensions, such as having sex.)

The good news – masturbation, sexual fantasies and having an imaginative and fertile solo sexual life don't mean you are sex obsessed. Good reasons to masturbate are: it feels good, it's a great way to learn about your body, it releases sexual tension and it's a good way to be sexual without having sex. Of course, masturbation is a preference and not everyone wants to do it, especially some girls who think it's 'dirty', but the fact is it's normal and it happens and if you're doing it it's completely fine.

Good touching/bad touching

You fancy the pants off each other so have already probably progressed from a quick kiss on the lips to French kissing (kissing with tongues), hands up tops and down pants,
also known as foreplay. Though called foreplay, it's worth
noting that just because it's literally the stuff you do to get
excited/aroused before having sex, it doesn't have to lead to
sex. On it's own it's a perfectly good way to have fun and
reach orgasm. Which brings us to the subject of good
touching and bad touching. This is a term that comes from
Holland and refers to touching that you like and want,
and touching that happens against your will. (With
younger kids good touching/bad touching is a great way to
get them to understand the concept that no-one is allowed
to touch their body in ways they don't like.)

Of course, in a relationship it can be hard to differenti-
ate between the two, but remember, wherever you are in
your relationship, if something feels too much or too
uncomfortable just say no to it. For instance, you might be
OK with kissing and touching each other's sex parts,
including breasts, penis and vaginal areas, but don't like the
idea of oral sex (see below). If so, say so, as sometimes people you're with will think you're into it just because you
haven't said you're not. Again, like the pressure to have
sex, it pays to stand up for yourself when you feel pushed
into touching that isn't enjoyable, as this is a classic way to
end up regretting what's happened the morning after.

With foreplay, one important thing to bear in mind is pre-ejaculate or pre-cum. This is when a guy's body gets aroused, the penis gets erect and prepares to pass semen, and fluid called pre-ejaculate seeps from the top of the penis. Though this is not semen, it may still contain a small amount of sperm and can still cause a girl to get pregnant if the head of the penis or the fluid comes into contact with the vagina. Which is why a condom needs to be slapped on right away when a boy is erect even if you're not going the whole way.

Oral sex

Do you really want to go there? This is the first question you should be asking yourself before you try oral sex. While it can be a big turn on, it's just one aspect of sex and not for everyone. If you're going to do it, it involves a lot of communication and consent to make it work. This is because, apart from being a very intimate sex act (and one that carries a risk of STIs – see Chapter 6 for more on this), lots of people are worried about doing it wrong or about smells or gagging. If this is your fear, bear in mind that there are no rules. You don't have to do it if the thought turns your stomach, but if you want to do it bear in mind the following:

Oral sex on a boy

Blow jobs, giving head or going down are just some of the names for this sex act, when a man's penis is kissed, licked or sucked by his partner. (Despite the name, no blowing is involved.) If you're going to try it, always do what you feel comfortable with and stop when you don't. If you're worried about the taste, relax. Semen is a mix of sperm, protein, sugars and fluid and though it can taste a bit odd – sometimes it's salty, other times it's affected by what your boyfriend's eaten – it's nothing to get hysterical about. Next, while you obviously can't get pregnant via oral sex, a sexually transmitted infection can be passed this way (see Chapter 6). Finally, to spit or swallow – if this is your worry, bear in mind you don't have to swallow if you don't want to. Just keep some tissues nearby and spit if he comes in your mouth. Try to do it politely – after all, it's not sexy to come up making gagging faces or spitting on the floor. If you don't want this to happen, ask your boyfriend to look out for signs that he's going to ejaculate. Just before he does his hips should retract a little, his penis will swell and contort, and his balls will move closer to the body. If you can't spot physical signs, then listen to his breathing and note how his movements speed up.

Oral sex on a girl

Many women and girls would quite happily give oral sex but feel weird about receiving cunnilingus (where the vagina and clitoris are stimulated using the tongue and mouth) from their boyfriends. Popular worries include: fears that your genitals smell; fears he doesn't really want to do it; and fears that you have odd-looking genitalia. The good news is that none of the above is true. While the vagina does have a natural musty smell, it's not disgusting. As for the look of your genitalia – don't worry: like your eyes, ears and nose, everyone's bits look different.

FIRST-TIME SEX – LET'S GET PHYSICAL

Don't you just hate it when you read a sex-education book and all it does is warn you against having sex and tell you how babies are made? Where's the part where sex is talked about in more depth – literally how to do it, how it feels and how to make it all easier? Well, here it is. It's essential to discuss it because it's so easy just to talk your way around sex and never get to the crux of the issue – the actually doing it part – which is what most people want to know about. Some teenagers feel that first-time sex was a huge disappointment because they weren't prepared for what it would be like. Take Kerry, who says, 'It hurt and then I thought, "What's the big deal?" People say sex is supposed to be good, but it really hurt. Not worth it really.' And Dionne, aged sixteen, who says, 'It really hurt the first time and I felt scared about it, scared about what would happen and what the outcome would be. I didn't realize you start bleeding after your first time and I thought I'd hurt myself or something.' So if you think you're alone in wondering what happens when two people have sex, here's what you need to know.

What's the best way to have sex?

There's no best way to have sex (besides ensuring you use contraception) and even though you may have heard talk of death-defying positions and elaborate skills, there are no special techniques or pretzel-like positions that you need to wrap your body into to make sex fantastic. Great sex comes when you and your partner are in a loving relationship and you know them well enough to understand what he/she likes – how they like to be kissed, talked to and touched. So much focus is put on the actual intercourse bit (where the penis is inserted into the vagina if it's heterosexual sex), but it's the stuff that you do before that counts. As eighteen-year-old Rory says, 'You need a lot of foreplay before you have sex otherwise it's pointless. You need to get them warmed up. A lot of foreplay definitely – kissing and touching and stuff.'

How do I do it?

Well, if you're straight – i.e. heterosexual – once foreplay has started and you're both into that, you'll find yourselves getting sexually excited. As this happens the penis will get erect and hard and the vagina will become moist, the girl's breasts will become sensitive and you'll feel your heartbeat quicken. When vaginal intercourse happens (and you can be in a variety of positions for this – lying down, standing up, etc.), the penis is inserted into the vagina. From this point a variety of things can happen: either ejaculation occurs (the release of semen due to a boy reaching the peak of excitement), or the guy will start a movement known as thrusting (where he moves backwards and forwards) to increase his excitement and ensure ejaculation happens. If you're a gay male, sex can take many other forms, such as foreplay, oral sex, mutual masturbation and in some cases anal sex to reach ejaculation and orgasm; if you're a gay woman, sex includes foreplay, oral sex and mutual masturbation as a way to orgasm.

What does it feel like?

If you're having sex with someone you trust and have taken time to get to this point of your relationship, sex can feel amazing – though it's worth noting that first-time sex can also be a bit painful. This happens for three reasons: lack of lubrication from not enough foreplay; nerves, which can cause muscles in the vaginal area to tense up and so the penis literally can't enter the vagina; or the hymen (the thin membrane over the entrance to the vagina) breaks on penetration, in which case you may notice a little blood. If things hurt, slow down or stop. Nothing beats putting sex on hold if it's not working and talking things over. It's not a race to get to the end and you don't have to go from 0 to 60 in one go if things go wrong or feel wrong. The good thing about sex is there's always tomorrow to try again.

How can I make it a good experience?

By having realistic expectations. You may have a great fantasy in your head about what sex will be like, but nine times out of ten it's going to be different to that. Real sex can be embarrassing, messy and noisy, which is why having a sense of humour and a level of honesty with your partner helps immensely. Understanding your body and how it works (as in what feels nice when it's touched in a certain way) is also a good way to make the experience more enjoyable and maybe even lead to orgasm (to know you're having one, look for a range of pulsating muscle spasms in the genital area during sex). Other ways to make it a good experience are to ensure that you're in a loving relationship, you're not doing it in the back of a car, or where you're likely to be spotted, and that you've got contraception covered. There's nothing more likely to lead to morning-after regrets and a bad first-time experience than worrying whether you're pregnant or have caught something nasty.

What is safe sex?

The only 100 per cent safe sex there is – is no sex. Safer sex is, therefore, sex where you ensure you protect yourself from an unplanned pregnancy and STIs by using the right type of barrier contraception (see below), which stops fluids from another person entering your body. It's also about not engaging in risky sexual behaviour – i.e. sleeping around and having unprotected sex with other people.

How long does it take to have sex?

It varies. It can take less than a minute, four minutes, forty minutes or even a couple of hours. Sex doesn't just mean intercourse; it also includes foreplay, afterplay and kissing, so when people say they were at it for hours they don't literally mean they were having intercourse for hours!

SAFER SEX AND CONTRACEPTION

'Double Dutch' is a fantastic phrase from Holland. All Dutch teenagers are aware of it. It means using the condom and the pill together when you're having sex to ensure that you avoid both sexually transmitted infections and pregnancy. It would be great for us if it caught on here, alongside a slogan that says 'No condom. No sex.' Holland has one of the lowest teenage pregnancy rates in Europe and Dutch teenagers are incredibly level headed about protecting themselves. Over here we seem to have a much more haphazard attitude towards contraception. Again, it's meant to be explained in schools, but it seems that many people come away with only some of the information they need, or have no idea where to go for advice and help.

Dionne was sixteen when she became pregnant. The only contraception she and her boyfriend had used was the belief that it wouldn't happen to them – and she's not alone. In the UK we have the highest rate of underage pregnancies in Western Europe and rocketing rates of sexually transmitted infections. Dionne was on the pill, but she stopped taking it when it didn't work for her. 'My periods were irregular – I used to have one every six months. As for condoms, he didn't like wearing them, so we didn't use them either. I didn't realize there were loads of different pills and I could have used something else. I thought there was just one.'

Contraception is all about choices. Not the choice of whether to go bareback (i.e. without a condom), or cross your fingers and think 'It won't happen to me,' but the choice of what to use, what not to use and how to protect yourself. So what do you really know about contraception? 'The pill protects me from everything,' or 'Condoms work every time,' or 'He's a nice guy and he's only had one other girlfriend so I won't catch anything from him.' If this is your line of thinking, you need to get informed.

If you want information, speak to your parents (if you can), ask the school nurse (if you have one) or go along to any young person's clinic (see Resources) and find out what works for you.

Confidentiality and contraceptives

Apart from condoms, which can be bought at a variety of places, and emergency contraception, which can be bought over the counter in pharmacies or obtained for free from drop-in health clinics, all other methods of contraception have to be prescribed by a GP or at a family-planning clinic or young person's clinic. The number-one fear that seems to stop many young people using contraception or seeking advice and help is the idea that, the second you see your doctor or a clinic, your confidentiality will be broken and your parents will be called.

The good news is that, under current guidelines for doctors and health professionals, under-sixteens are entitled to confidential treatment – though there is flexibility in this area. If doctors or health professionals believe you are mature enough to understand what's happening and what you are asking for, they will not breach confidentiality. If, though, they believe there is a serious threat to your health or something is not right (such as there has been a rape or some sort of abuse), they can choose to break it. However, whatever their decision, the emphasis will always be to encourage you to speak to your parents.

WHAT'S NOT CONTRACEPTION

Before we head into the world of what you can use to protect yourself, here's a quick word about what doesn't work. No matter how informed you think you are, myths abound, so here's what to watch out for:

Withdrawal

This is where a guy withdraws his penis before ejaculating, thereby aiming to leave no sperm inside a girl. The problem with this method is that it's virtually impossible to do simply because pre-ejaculatory semen contains sperm, so sperm gets in even if you don't ejaculate. Plus – and this is a biggie – withdrawal is hard to time when you're not used to your body. Withdrawal also offers no protection against sexually transmitted infections, which means even if an unplanned pregnancy doesn't happen an infection is still on the cards.

Peeing after sex

Again, this is based on the idea that a girl can literally expel all semen by peeing. It's a total myth because semen is expelled far into the vagina and sperm swim at a super-fast speed (if a sperm were the size of a salmon it would be swimming its 17.5-centimetre journey at 500 miles per hour!). It's therefore 100 per cent unreliable.

Douching

This is where a girl washes herself out so she can get rid of sperm – again, it doesn't work. Also, vaginal douching is unhealthy as it changes the chemical balance of the vagina. It can therefore make a woman more susceptible to infections as it can introduce new bacteria into the vagina, which can spread up through the cervix, uterus and fallopian tubes. Researchers have found that women who douche regularly experience more vaginal irritations and infections such as bacterial vaginosis (see Chapter 6), and an increased number of sexually transmitted infections.

Having sex on your period

Many women believe that having unprotected sex during menstruation or during the first or last part of their menstrual cycle will keep them from becoming pregnant. The problem is that sperm hangs about for around five to seven days, which means you could well ovulate (release an egg) early and get pregnant a few days later, so it's a very unsafe method.

Sex in various positions

Standing up, standing on your head, on top, against a wall – it doesn't matter: it's still sex and you can still get pregnant.

If it's the first time you've had sex

If you have started your periods, you can get pregnant! What's more, younger girls are more fertile than older women and can get pregnant very easily. It's also worth bearing in mind that you can get pregnant before starting your periods, especially if you have started puberty, because you never know the exact point at which you will ovulate and your periods will begin.

If you forget to take your pill

The pill only works efficiently if you remember to take it every day. Be slack about this and it simply won't work. And while we're on the subject, doubling up the day after doesn't help!

Even if it's quick

Sex, no matter how fast, is still sex – meaning, even if it lasts no longer than thirty seconds, if sperm is ejaculated into your vagina without protection you can get pregnant!

Why you should use contraception

Of the approximately 42,000 girls under eighteen who get pregnant every year, around 8,000 are under sixteen and many of these girls probably never thought it would happen to them. Part of the problem is that around the age of fifteen or sixteen, girls are super-fertile.

In addition to not getting pregnant, here are a few more reasons why you should use contraception:

- It's easier than dealing with a horrible growth on your genitals.
- It's free and easy to get hold of.
- It's easier than worrying about the worst.

- It will protect the sexual health of the person you love as well as your own.
- It will keep you fertile.
- It will help keep sex pain-free.
- It will stop you infecting future lovers.
- It will stop you passing on infections to your baby when you're ready to have one.

'I found out about the pill from my mum – she was on it. Then I went with my mates to a clinic to get it done properly, so they could take my blood pressure and stuff, and I got the pill up there. Microgynon they gave me, but it made me go mental and so I went to the doctors and they gave me a different pill – Celeste. I've been on it for two years now. But with my boyfriend we're using the pill and condoms – it protects you from everything.'

KERRY, 16

WHAT IS CONTRACEPTION?

The Pill

 The pill is a hormonal method of contraception, which contains two hormones – oestrogen and progestogen – which prevent an egg from being released by a woman's ovaries each month. This means the pill basically tricks your body into thinking you are pregnant, so your own hormones aren't released to start up your menstrual cycle. Alongside this, the pill activates the build-up of what's known as cervical mucus so sperm cannot get through and a fertilized egg (if there is one) cannot implant itself in the womb lining.

It is highly effective when used properly but offers no protection against STIs. It's estimated that 3.5 million women in the UK take the pill, simply because it's the most foolproof method of contraception available.

Pill facts

- There are many different types of pills, so even if one doesn't work for you because it gives you side-effects, go back to your GP and ask for another one.
- The pill is more likely to benefit your general health than damage it. In fact, it will not only improve your skin, reduce period cramping and heavy blood loss, but it will also help you to stay fertile longer.
- It's also worth knowing that today's pills are safer than ever. They have much lower dosages of hormones, and

some even carry only one type of hormone, all of which helps combat the various side-effects, such as nausea and headaches.

- Most pill packs are designed to last a month and every pill contains exactly the same amount of hormone. You take one pill every day for three weeks and then you take a week off (with some brands you have to take placebo pills during this week). During this week off, the womb lining will be expelled and you get a period, though not a 'real' period because ovulation has not occurred.

The Pill health bonuses
- Regular periods.
- Less or no cramping.
- Clearer skin.
- Lower incidence of breast cancer, ovarian cancer, endometrial cancer.
- Lower risk of pelvic inflammatory disease.
- Fewer ovarian cysts.
- May help to preserve fertility.
- Builds stronger bones.
- Reduces heavy bleeding from periods.
- Reduces iron-deficiency anaemia.
- Stops you getting pregnant.

Pill myths
- It makes you fat. Weight gain, if there is any, usually occurs only in the first month as your body adjusts to the contraceptive. If weight gain continues, it's likely you need to be on a different pill, with a different hormonal dosage.

- It's bad for you to go directly from one pack to the next, without taking a week off for a period. Strangely enough, there is nothing necessary about this 'period'. In the early days, the pill was developed to copy the menstrual cycle because manufacturers believed most women would still want to take a pill that allowed them to mimic the natural 28-day cycle. This means you can safely take the pill without a monthly bleed, though you should always check with your GP first.
- The pill gives you lots of side-effects like nausea and headaches. Some pills can give you side-effects (but bear in mind all drugs and medicines can give you side-effects), but lots of women have none. If you're suffering, see your doctor in order to change to a pill with a different hormonal dosage.
- Taking more than one will give you double protection. Taking a double dose will not give you double protection.

Condoms

 The Science Bit... Condoms are made of very thin latex rubber and work by being placed over the penis. They act as a physical barrier and trap sperm at the point of ejaculation. They help to protect against cancer of the cervix and reduce the risk of STIs, including chlamydia and HIV.

Condom facts

- The condom will protect you from STIs and pregnancy.
- Only ever use water-based lubricants such as KY Jelly with condoms. Vaseline, body oils and lotions can erode latex, making it tear easily.
- Always store condoms in a cool place; heat also erodes latex.

How to use a condom

- Don't tear the packet open with your teeth, and watch sharp nails and jewellery – condoms, while tough, do snag easily on sharp things.
- Do not roll on a condom until the penis is erect.
- Do not unravel one and attempt to place it over a flaccid penis.
- Squeeze the tip to get rid of the air, place the condom on the head of the penis and gently roll it down over the penis to the base, smoothing out bubbles as you go (air bubbles can cause the condom to break during sex).
- Ensure a man withdraws as soon as possible after ejaculation, holding the condom in place at the base so that it doesn't slip off and semen doesn't slip out.
- Never re-use a condom.
- If a condom splits, tears or slips off inside you, always make sure you get advice or emergency contraception from your GP or a sexual health clinic.

'I use condoms because you don't know what's going round. My mates don't really care.'

FEMI, 18

'I don't want to go on the pill because it made my mum fat. I don't want the injection and my mum's told me about the whole coil thing. I don't know about the female condom and what you do with it. We have a booklet downstairs on contraception and I was reading it the other night and weighing up all the options. The condoms seemed like the best option.'

STEPHANIE, 15

Condom myths

- It makes sex uncomfortable. Not true – condoms are ultra thin and once stretched over an erect penis do not hinder sex or ejaculation.
- Most men find them too tight. Highly unlikely – blow one up like a balloon and you'll really see how far they stretch.
- They don't work anyway. Totally untrue – use them properly (see instructions above) and they work very effectively. In fact, if used according to instructions, condoms are 98 per cent effective (the 2 per cent is often down to human error).

IUD (Intrauterine Device) or Coil

This small plastic and copper device, usually shaped like a 'T' or '7', works from the moment it is placed in the uterus and can stay in place for five years. The only problem is that some IUDs may cause periods to be heavier and sometimes the womb can also expel the IUD. If this occurs you will be at risk of pregnancy as soon as you have sex. It is 98–9 per cent effective.

Gynefix is another type of IUD. It has a short row of copper beads which bend to fit the inside of the uterus, instead of being 'T'-shaped like most IUDs. Once properly inserted it causes fewer painful side-effects than traditional IUDS and can be used either as a long-term contraceptive, staying in place for five years, or as an emergency method of contraception within five days of unprotected intercourse. It is 99 per cent effective.

IUS (Intrauterine System)

This is a small plastic device containing the hormone progestogen. It is effective as soon as it is placed in the womb and lasts for at least three years. It can be very useful for women with painful, heavy periods as it makes periods lighter, but sporadic bleeding is common for the first three months and there may be temporary side-effects like acne and breast tenderness. It is 99 per cent effective.

Implant

An implant is a small soft tube, the size of a matchstick, which is placed under the skin of the upper arm. It then releases a steady flow of the hormone progestogen into the bloodstream. You are protected from pregnancy for up to five years, but implants are unsuitable for women who are at risk from stroke, heart disease, liver disease, or breast or ovarian cancer. It is 99 per cent effective in the first year of use and 98 per cent effective over five years.

Contraceptive injection

This is an injection of hormones that provides a longer-acting alternative to the pill. It works by slowly releasing the hormone progestogen into the body to stop ovulation. It is injected into a muscle, usually in your bottom.

You don't have to think about contraception for as long as the injection lasts, but possible side-effects include weight gain and irregular bleeding. The most popular form of this type of contraception, Depo-Provera, involves a girl having an injection once every twelve weeks. It has the advantage that you do not have to remember to take a pill every day but it provides no protection against sexually transmitted infections. It is 99 per cent effective.

Female condom

Known as the Femidom, the female condom is a tube-like appliance with rings at either end. The small end fits into the vagina and the big end hangs outside the vagina, so that the whole vagina is protected. Some people complain it's like having sex inside a bag, but the truth is the female condom is made of very thin polyurethane and as long as it is held in place during penetration he will not slip under it and it won't slip when he withdraws. It is 98 per cent effective.

NOT TEEN-FRIENDLY

Diaphragm/Cap
The diaphragm is a circular dome made of rubber that is used with spermicidal cream and fitted over the cervix to stop sperm from getting into the uterus. You can put it in any time before sex, but a trained nurse must initially fit it. Fitting should be checked every year, and/or if you gain or lose weight or have a baby. The diaphragm is 96 per cent effective.

Natural methods
(the rhythm method, the basal body temperature method, the Billings/cervical mucus method)
This is a form of contraception where a woman counts the days when she will be fertile and the days when she will not. She must then avoid sex (or use a method of contraception) on fertile days. It's very hard to do: you have to be very conscientious and have a regular cycle. There are no harmful side-effects, but if you're not disciplined there is a very high failure rate.

Sponge
The sponge works by releasing spermicidal gel over the vaginal mucus while the sponge itself forms a barrier to kill or immobilize sperm before they can reach the cervix and enter the uterus. The sponge can be inserted several hours before intercourse and can be left in place up to twelve hours after sex. It does not need to be replaced if sexual intercourse is repeated but is only 90 per cent effective.

Emergency contraception

This used to be known as the morning-after pill, but the name has changed to emergency contraception so that people become aware that it works for longer than the morning-after period (though the sooner you sort it out the more effective the contraceptive will be). There are two methods of preventing pregnancy after unprotected sex and both have to be started within one to five days:

Emergency pill (ECP)

This is available from your local chemist, your GP and family-planning clinics/young people's clinics. If taken within seventy-two hours (three days) of unprotected sex, the emergency contraceptive pill can stop a pregnancy. However, it is not the same as the abortion pill. ECP stops conception occurring; it won't work if you are already pregnant, unlike the abortion pill, which stops a pregnancy happening and isn't available from pharmacists because it's not a method of contraception.

Unlike PC4 – the old emergency pill – which contained four pills and was available only on prescription, the current ECP, Levonelle-2, has only two pills. The benefits of this pill are:

- It doesn't make you feel sick or cause you to throw up.
- It's also 95 per cent effective and holds no health risks.

The pill contains a female-type hormone called 'lev-onorgestrel', which is one of the ingredients of several types of contraceptive pill and is believed to work principally by either preventing your ovaries from releasing an egg or by affecting the womb lining so that a fertilized egg couldn't 'embed' itself there.

IUD

If you've waited beyond seventy-two hours but less than five days, an IUD can be inserted into the uterus by a doctor at any family-planning clinic or young person's clinic to prevent the lining of the womb from thickening and therefore halt conception. This is an effective post-sex method and its contraceptive value can last three years (or you can have it removed again).

Coming soon – the male pill

This method, currently undergoing clinical trial, will actually not be a pill but an injection and an implant under the skin. The injection contains a synthetic form of a hormone that occurs naturally in women but which effectively halts sperm production in men. It also turns off testosterone production, so an implant containing synthetic testosterone will also be required. The injection will be required every three months, and the implants need replacing every four months. Trials suggest it is 100 per cent effective in protecting against pregnancy and has no serious side-effects. However, it does not protect against sex infections and you would also have to trust someone completely to believe them when they said they had an implant/injection. Plus it will be years before a male hormonal contraceptive becomes widely available on the market.

POST-SEX WORRIES

'What's next' is usually the first fear that comes to mind for most people when thinking about life after sex. 'Do we do it every time from now on?' or 'is that it?' The problem is that if you have sex for the first time without talking about life after sex, you could be in for some nasty surprises such as one of you thinking that sex is on the menu all the time, or the other assuming it was a one-off. Not only that, but what about your post-sex emotions? The morning after the night before can be joyous and happy for some, but if you have sex without taking precautions, for the wrong reasons or with someone you're not sure of you can end up feeling sad, embarrassed, ashamed, and even angry with yourself once sex is over. The post-sex world is a place that is rich in misunderstandings, which is why you need to think about all your potential post-sex worries, before having sex. Some things to consider and discuss with your partner are:

Keeping sex private

Girls in particular are guilty of sharing way too much with their friends about their love lives, and while you may not do it to boast about your sex life it's still unfair to pass on private information about what's occurred within your relationship. Likewise, some boys boast about their conquests and need a good shaking. If you're both ready for sex, then you're both ready to keep certain issues private and between you only. Talk in advance about what can and can't be said, and who can and can't be told. And bear in mind that if you don't trust your partner or don't trust yourself to keep quiet, you could be having sex for all the wrong reasons.

'Men boast about sex. I think it's something that men do. They boast about everything. It's not just about sex, it's about everything. It's to make you feel good. All guys are in a big competition, trying to see who does the best. I don't really talk about my sex life with my friends. Before I used to, but when I got into a relationship I realized my sex life is my sex life.'

FEMI, 18

Double standards: 'men' versus 'slags'

He's a sex god because he's done it and she's a 'slag' because she's done it. We've all seen this nasty double standard in action, usually fuelled by someone's boasting about his conquests to boost his standing amongst his friends, or a girl's being punished by jealous peers or stupid boys for daring to do what boys are congratulated for doing. Double standards persist because we let them. If you hear someone saying girls are easy for having sex, then stand up for what you believe in. Point out the ridiculousness of the double standard and turn the tables on whoever is saying it. It's a stupid belief, because sex is just sex and it has the same repercussions for us all.

What will my parents say?

If you get caught doing it at home, or at school, or even behind a bush, they'll probably have quite a lot to say, but if you plan where you're going to have sex so it's a safe place where you're unlikely to be disturbed, being caught shouldn't be a worry.

If you decide to tell your parents, be sure to say you have practised safe sex and have had sex for the right reasons, maybe even listing a few of them. Of course, they may be disappointed because no-one wants to think their children are having sex, or shocked because they waited and/or just assumed you wouldn't have sex for quite a while yet. Or maybe they will be angry as it goes against their religious/cultural values, in which case it's up to you to decide what information is appropriate to pass their way. Whatever you decide, bear in mind that your parents are a rich source of support when it comes to sex and relationships, so while you may not want to spill all with them (and they may not want you to tell them everything), don't stop talking just because you're having sex. Keep the lines of communication open, because even though you've decided to have sex, that's not the end of the information and help they can pass on.

What if I hated it?

There's no law that says if you don't like it you still have to do it. The key is to be honest and not let yourself be bullied into a sex life that you don't want. Some people believe you can't go back to holding hands after having sex, but of course you can. It's your body and your decision. Though remember, first-time sex is rarely pleasurable for anyone. It takes time, effort and a fantastic relationship to learn to give and receive pleasure. Take your time: if you're meant to be together, you can easily slow down and wait a while before you jump into it again.

YOUR QUESTIONS ANSWERED

Q I am fifteen years old and in love with a boy who is also fifteen. We've been together for a year and everyone we know reckons we're a great couple. I love him, and though we kiss and touch and stuff we haven't had sex yet. He wants to but is not pushing me, but my friends say it's time and that he may leave me if I don't do it soon because the other girls are all doing it. The problem is, I can't tell if I'm ready. How do I know?

A Just like knowing when you're in love and knowing when you've done well in an exam, you will just know deep inside when you're ready to have sex. You'll feel comfortable with your decision, and feel it's 100 per cent right for you and your partner. The fact that you're wavering and being pushed into it by your friends suggests that you're not ready yet. It doesn't matter if the whole world around you is having sex, or that someone says he'll leave you if you don't do it; if you're not ready, don't give in. Mind you, it's not your boyfriend exerting the pressure here, it's your friends – and apart from its being none of their business, what do they really know? They may have had relationships that depended on whether they had sex or not, but you obviously don't, so don't let them make you feel insecure about what is obviously a great relationship.

Also bear in mind that if you have sex before the age of sixteen you will be breaking the law.

Q My girlfriend and I are both sixteen and are planning to have sex in a few weeks. We've talked about it for ages and have got contraception and even sorted out where we're going to do it (at her place, as her parents are away). She's really happy about it and keeps talking about what it will be like and what might happen. All her talk is making me nervous. What if I can't get it up, and how will I know what to do for her? She thinks I am experienced but I'm a virgin like her. I told her I wasn't because girls don't like it if you don't know what you're doing. Help!

A It doesn't bode well on the trust front that you're leading your girlfriend to believe you have had sex when you haven't. Your virginal status shouldn't matter to her seeing as she cares about you, and it shouldn't matter to you seeing as she's not making a big deal about it. While you may think there is a pressure to be macho and have a long list of conquests, the reality is it's not that appealing to girls – so tell her the truth before you have sex. The upside of confessing all is that you can then both explore sex together with the same level of comfort and knowledge. As for worries about performance, just relax and enjoy the moment. Stress about not getting an erection and the pressure to get it up will intensify. To find out what to do for her during sex, the key is communication. Remember, you're having sex; this doesn't mean you can't speak. Ask her what she likes and dislikes as you go along. If she's too embarrassed to speak, listen out for hints that she likes what you're doing (smiles and noises) and hints that she doesn't (moving away from you).

Q My boyfriend and I are worried. I am fourteen and he's fifteen and we're thinking about having sex but know it's against the law. Does this mean if we go along and try to get contraception from the doctor's or a clinic we'll get caught and arrested or our parents will be called? And what if we just buy condoms – can someone refuse to sell them to us? A friend suggested we use one of her pills and I am tempted, but is this dangerous? My boyfriend says if the worst comes to the worst he'll just pull out, but I've heard this doesn't always work.

A Yes, if you have sex you will be breaking the law as you are under the age of consent; however, this doesn't mean you will be arrested if you try to get contraception. The guide-lines for doctors are clear and state that help can be given to under-sixteens as long as they are deemed mature enough to understand what's being said. Even if they don't think you are, which is rare, they won't just call your parents but will suggest you go home and talk to them, so your confidentiality is still protected. Whatever you decide to do, don't be tempted by DIY contraception methods. Borrowing someone's pill won't work and neither will withdrawal. The pill has to be prescribed so that you get a type that's right for you. A course then has to be taken over a month so that it works effectively. If you're serious that you're ready to have sex, be serious about what contraception you're going to use and seek out professional help and advice at a young person's clinic (see Brook in Resources) before doing anything.

Q Last night I got drunk at a party and ended up having a one-night stand with a friend. I don't remember much apart from the condom broke at the end. I was a virgin at the time and now really hate myself for what happened. I wanted to wait until I met someone special and now I've ruined it all. I feel cheap and really guilty, especially as my mum would be really upset if she found out. She's always been open with me and honest, and I said I'd wait until I was older (I am sixteen). What have I done?

A You haven't done anything evil, you've simply made a mistake like lots of people do and you need to stop giving yourself a hard time about it. Instead, learn from what happened so that you can avoid a repeat incident the next time. As for your mum finding out – yes, she may be disappointed, but she wouldn't want you to think so badly of yourself and punish yourself over and over. You're not cheap and have nothing to feel guilty about – keep telling yourself this and all that will happen is you'll begin to believe it. On a practical note, the sex you had was unprotected as the condom broke, so you need to get emergency contraception as soon as possible from a young person's clinic (see Brook and FPA in Resources). The doctor will either give you the emergency pill, which can be taken within seventy-two hours, or the IUD, which can be fitted up to five days after unprotected sex.

6

THE UNPLANNED STUFF

SEXUALLY TRANSMITTED INFECTIONS AND PREGNANCY

'I am appalled at the lack of knowledge in the young people I see in the STI clinic. Obviously, most of them who end up there have already caught something and they are absolute proof of the hopelessness of the sexual and relationship education that they received. Some have even no idea about contraception, many have never heard of chlamydia, and they have some of the strangest notions about HIV and who can catch it. Isn't it a shame that they have to wait to catch a sexually transmitted infection before they start finding out about it?'

DR COLM O'MAHONY

Let's face it, most kids would rather cross their fingers and hope for the best than have a discussion with you about how to protect their sexual health, because, as we all know, when thinking about sex for the first time infections and pregnancy are not at the forefront of anyone's mind. And that's the problem with sexual health: no-one really thinks about it until they have to – i.e. when they possibly have something to worry about. So while the basic biology is covered under the National Curriculum, it's crucial that you also talk about sexual health at home because detail is often lacking and subjects such as confidentiality, where to go for help, how STIs are spread and what to do if you think you've caught an infection can be missed and/or ignored.

This is why thousands of young people play Russian roulette with their future sexual health every day, and why the statistics are so alarming. If you don't believe me, then look at the figures. Around 800,000 STIs a year are diagnosed at genito-urinary medicine (GUM) clinics (and that's just the people who go to get checked out). Each year in the UK around 42,000 girls under eighteen get pregnant. Of these, around 8,000 are under sixteen.

Part of the problem is that so many people (and not just teenagers) think they are immune when it comes to unplanned pregnancies or STIs and assume that, because they've risked it and been lucky once or twice, it will just never happen to them. Take Femi and James. Femi, aged eighteen, uses condoms but says, 'I use them because you don't know what's going around, but my mates don't really care. But really they're at a very low risk because most people they go with we've known for a long time. I'm sure if they had any STIs they would know about it.' James, also eighteen, on the other hand often doesn't often use condoms. His view is, he will only use a condom if a partner asks. He says, 'I know I'm at risk of getting STIs but it's not as common as people think. I haven't been for an STI test because I don't believe I have anything' (James was later diagnosed with chlamydia). Then there's sixteen-year-old Dionne who got pregnant because she didn't understand fully how the pill worked and didn't realize conception could happen so quickly.

So how do you talk to a teenager who really just wants to know about the good side of sex? Well, the only way to do it is to give them the plain facts, gory details and all, and on a fairly repetitive basis so it sinks in. The key is to emphasize how having unprotected sex is like a game of dare. Each time you play, you walk in blind and take your chances on what might happen. The result could be a lucky escape (which, let's face it, is a double-edged sword because it just tempts you to keep taking chances until you lose), an unplanned pregnancy, a lifelong infection, sores or a tantalizing mixture of all the above.

To help your kids get their heads around sexual-health issues and the necessity always to go Double Dutch (condom and pill), the rest of this chapter is written directly to them. However, it is also full of information for you, so as tricky and as full of medical stuff as it is, don't be tempted to skip it.

TIPS FOR TALKING TO YOUR TEENS

Stay informed

Sexual health is a confusing subject, not to mention one where the facts on tests, transmission and prevention differ and sometimes change. To feel confident about what you say, stay informed (see Resources for good sex education sites) by reading up on the infections that may not have been mentioned when you were young – such as chlamydia – and new tests and vaccines (such as the new cervical cancer vaccine covered later in this chapter) that will be available soon.

Find out what your kids already know

As always, an excellent place to start so you can find out what their knowledge base is and what needs to be filled in. Is their information correct? What areas need to be explained more fully and what myths, if any, do they believe about pregnancy and STIs?

Talk about responsibility

That is, responsibility to look after themselves and their partners, and responsibility to practise safe sex, and to get checked out if they don't.

Talk to them, whether they're having sex or not

It's never too early or too late to talk to your children about STIs and unplanned pregnancies. Even if they have been having sex it still pays to find out if they're being safe and what they know about the above, because whatever they know now (or don't know) they'll take into adulthood.

Give them the real facts
Don't soften the facts, but at the same time don't overdo it – otherwise they'll ignore the dangers or assume you're exaggerating and switch off. The aim is to give them a balanced view of what can happen with unprotected sex so that they want to protect themselves and their partners.

THE OTHER SIDE OF THE COIN
Sexual Health

What does practising good sexual health really mean? Well, apart from having safe sex to avoid nasty lumps and bumps on your sexual parts, good sexual health is also about being hygienic. Which means learning to be spotlessly clean in every nook and cranny; after all, nothing is more of a turn off than unpleasant whiffs in the pants department! That aside, sexual health is also about looking after your well-being by ensuring that you have the right tests and do the right examinations to make sure you're free from infection and disease all the way through your sexual life. Sometimes this will be about going to a genito-urinary medicine clinic (specialists in STI diagnosis and treatment); other times about going to your GP (for smear tests); and checking your body yourself on a regular basis (testicular examinations and breast examinations). In addition to that, here's what you need to know about STIs, unplanned pregnancies and other infections you may encounter.

What are STIs?

Sexually transmitted infections are a whole host of genital nasties that are basically transmitted via unprotected sex. They used to be known as sexually transmitted diseases or venereal diseases – as well as the clap and other slang words; call them what you may, they are highly contagious and therefore very easy to get. The problem is, you may think you can afford to have unprotected sex on one occasion, but if the person you're having sex with has also had unprotected sex once before, say with someone who also has had unprotected sex, and so on and so on, you're actually coming into contact with hundreds of other people via just one sexual encounter. This is exactly how STIs are spread and why you need always to practise safe sex.

How to avoid a sexually transmitted infection

The number-one way is to not have sex – but obviously that's a useless bit of advice if you're already having sex or planning on doing it at some point in your life. In which case you need to get your head around the following things.

The fact you can't tell by looking
Someone can be scrupulously clean and smell like roses but still have an STI because many STIs don't have symptoms.

This means they can promise you they don't have an infection because they honestly think they're clear, when in fact there could be a silent, unknown infection raging inside them.

Safe sex

This is sex with a condom. A condom is your best friend during sex because it protects you from a large variety of STIs as well as from pregnancy. So step one is to get used to handling a condom. You may think it's easy to put one on, but you'd be amazed at how many people get it wrong – try to roll it on inside out, tear it while they're putting it on, or even forget to hold on to it when they're withdrawing. The trick is to unravel a condom on an erect penis only, roll it down slowly and squeeze all the air bubbles out of it once it's on. When you're done with it, it needs to be held on the penis as the man withdraws so that it doesn't slip off.

Step two is to seek medical help asap if you suspect you have something or if the condom breaks. This may feel embarrassing (but, really, GUM doctors have seen it all, so don't worry) but it's worth doing for the sake of your health, your future partners and your chances of having a child in later life.

Monogamy

Also known as staying faithful and limiting your partners. Put it around and all you're doing is increasing your risk of catching an STI. If you're in a relationship, stay faithful – and if you can't do that always make sure you use a condom so you don't pass infections along or risk catching one yourself.

Being tested

Even if you've only ever had unprotected sex once and the person said they were a virgin, it pays to get tested, not only to put your own mind at rest but also your future partners', because there will come a time one day when you'll decide that you are in the right relationship and stop using contraception, and then who knows what you'll pass on.

How to get an STI

Sexually transmitted infections are passed only through sex and genital contact – that's either through infected blood, semen or vaginal fluids, which means unprotected sex is the culprit. Besides practising safe sex:

- Make sure you and a new partner are checked out and cleared of infection before you start having unprotected sex together.
- Always use a barrier method of contraception, like the condom, if you have sex with someone you don't know is clear, as this will literally block STIs.

Be aware that STIs don't always present symptoms, but signs to watch out for are:

- Mysterious genital lumps and bumps.
- Vaginal blisters – small or large.
- Discharges – watery, or lumpy or smelly.
- Irritation – anywhere in the genital region.
- Strange smells – especially if they're fishy.

- Rashes around the genital area (not just the vagina, but the bottom and upper thighs).
- Pain during sex – contrary to popular belief, this is not normal.
- Lumps, rashes and discharges from the penis.
- Painful urination.

Reasons why people get STIs

There are two main reasons why people usually get STIs: (a) they think it won't happen to them (if this is you, keep re-reading this chapter until it sinks in); or (b) they let themselves be persuaded into having unsafe sex. Like the pressure to have sex, the following are all things someone might say to get you to go bareback (have sex without a condom):

- 'I don't like the tight feel of condoms.' This is rubbish, as condoms are ultra-thin and, despite what some guys say, can stretch to amazing widths and lengths, so it will never be too small or too tight unless you're dating someone who should be in the *Guinness Book of Records*!
- 'I feel like condoms are like a barrier between good sex and us.' Again, utterly stupid – condoms are a barrier method (as that's the point of them) and condom use has nothing to do with how good (or bad) sex is.
- 'Are you saying I've got something?' A bit like the old 'If you loved me you'd have sex with me' comment, this is designed purely to make you feel bad and give in.
- 'No-one bothers with condoms.' Does this mean everyone they've slept with so far hasn't bothered? In which

case there's all the more reason to be very bothered.

- 'STIs aren't that common.' Yes they are!
- 'Showering and peeing right after gets rid of all the infections.' No it doesn't!

Getting help

If you're lucky there's a young person's clinic at your school or one near you that offers confidential help and advice from trained counsellors and nurses. Some of these clinics offer free condoms, emergency contraception and even pregnancy testing in a safe environment where there's no risk of anyone finding out you've been. If not, genito-urinary medicine (GUM) clinics are the very best places to go to if you need to get checked out for STIs. Also known as VD clinics and special clinics, they are 100 per cent confidential and are run by doctors who are sympathetic and non-judgemental. Most GUM clinics are found in hospitals and the good news is that the records held there never, ever leave the clinic. This means they are not placed with your normal hospital records or sent to your GP, so if you have a sexually transmitted infection no-one will ever know you've been to the clinic. The other good things about these clinics are that they will see you if you're under sixteen, you can take a friend with you for moral support, and you can ask to see a male or female doctor. To find a clinic call or go to:

- Sexwise – 0800 28 29 30 (7am–midnight)
  www.ruthinking.co.uk
  The website also helps you search for services for STIs, contraception and abortion anywhere in the UK.
- Look in your local phone directory or search the internet under genito-urinary medicine (GUM), sexually transmitted infection clinic.
- Call the fpa helpline on 0845 310 1334
  (Monday to Friday, 9am–6pm)
- Call NHS Direct on 0845 46 47 (24 hours)

What to do if you have an infection

If an STI has been diagnosed, make sure you avoid sex until you and your partner have both been treated for the infection and you have both been given the all-clear. Never assume that you're clear just because your symptoms have gone away, and always finish your whole course of medication and go back for a check-up test before having sex again.

Also, hard as it is to have to tell your partner (or an ex-partner) that you've got something, it's your responsibility to do so. Avoid telling the truth and all that will happen is you'll be re-infected when you have sex again and they'll go on unwittingly to infect others and maybe even risk their future chances of having children. It's a heavy load to carry just because you feel uncomfortable and maybe ashamed, so do the right thing.

SEXUALLY TRANSMITTED INFECTIONS

Chlamydia

One in ten women aged 16–25 are affected with chlamydia in the UK and the latest figures show that the number of cases identified at GUM clinics rose by a staggering 206 per cent between 1996 and 2005, with some studies showing that there are also a vast number of people who have chlamydia but are unaware that they are infected because they have no symptoms. A scary thought because, if left untreated, chlamydia can lead to pelvic inflammatory disease (PID) and possible infertility.

What are the symptoms?

The problem with chlamydia is that it produces no obvious symptoms in at least six out of ten people who are infected, but in some cases possible symptoms to look out for are: breakthrough bleeding between periods; vaginal bleeding after sex; abnormal discharge; pain when you pee; and in men a small milky discharge when peeing.

How is it treated?

Chlamydia is diagnosed with a simple swab test and then treated with antibiotics. It's vital not to resume sexual activity until treatment has finished and you're given the all clear, otherwise infection can be passed again between you and your partner, who must also be treated.

A microbe causes chlamydia, and in women the infection begins on the cervix, which means unless it is diagnosed and treated it spreads to the fallopian tubes (the tubes along which an egg passes to get to the womb) and results in pelvic inflammatory disease. It is PID that then leads to problems with fertility, as the fallopian tubes become blocked and scarred as a result of the disease and, once this occurs, fertilized eggs cannot reach the uterus and you may not be able to get pregnant. If you do get pregnant after PID, there is an increased risk of an ectopic pregnancy (where the fertilized egg starts developing in the fallopian tube rather than in the womb), which is highly dangerous and results in a termination. In men chlamydia usually presents no symptoms but can eventually cause inflammation in the testicles and sperm-conducting tubes. This causes pain, swelling and redness in the scrotum. Researchers from Sweden's Umea University have also found that chlamydia could reduce a man's fertility by a third.

HPV/genital warts (see also Cervical cancer)

HPV is the second most common sexually transmitted infection seen in GUM clinics in the UK, with 81,203 cases diagnosed in 2005. It's transmitted through sexual contact and, despite the idea that you'd obviously see the warts if you had them, many people are infected and don't know it. This is because most carriers do not have active warts, or the warts are so far inside you can't see them, so lack of visible warts on a sexual partner does not mean they're free from infection. Also, while using condoms helps to prevent transmission of the wart virus, it may not give total protection, as the condom may not cover all affected areas (for example, warts may be present on the scrotum and bottom).

How are genital warts treated?

For the quickest results, warts are destroyed by heat under local anaesthetic. A cream called Imiquimod can also be prescribed and has to be applied three times a week to the wart area before you go to sleep and is then washed off six to ten hours later (i.e. next morning). Treatment continues until the warts clear or for a maximum of sixteen weeks. Freezing with liquid nitrogen or cryotherapy also kills warts by disrupting and killing cells through repeated freezing then thawing, but several sessions are usually needed before the warts disappear.

 Warts can vary from small, multiple lumps to single, large growths and they can occur anywhere on the male and female genitals and anus. Once you're infected, the virus lies dormant in cells and the warts may appear from several weeks to twenty months afterwards. Even when warts are treated and disappear, the virus can still be found lying dormant in skin cells, so recurrences and transmission to others are common.

Herpes (HSV)

The Science Bit... There are two types of the herpes virus, *Herpes simplex-1*, which usually causes cold sores around the mouth and has nothing to do with sex; and *Herpes simplex-2*, which is a sexual infection and causes genital sores. The problem is, it's possible to pass *Herpes simplex-1* to your partner's genitals if you have cold sores and give your partner oral sex. Outside of this, to get herpes you have to touch skin that's infected, but again, infected skin doesn't always have sores, so once more your partner may look clear of herpes but won't necessarily be. Overall in 2005 there were 19,771 cases of genital herpes diagnosed at GUM clinics in the UK.

What are the symptoms?

Small burning or itching sensation, then blisters on the genital region, which eventually become sores, pain when passing urine, flu-like illness, and headaches.

How is it treated?

There is no cure for herpes and once the virus is in your body you can't get rid of it, meaning you can have regular flare-ups of sores. Treatment involves keeping outbreaks to the minimum with tablets, which will be given to reduce the HSV infection. One important fact to remember is that HSV is highly infectious and during an outbreak you should avoid sex and kissing entirely for two to three weeks until all sores have gone.

Gonorrhoea

Gonorrhoea is an infection that affects both men and women, and in five out of every six cases there are no symptoms. Between 1996 and 2005 there was a 55 per cent increase in cases reported at GUM clinics in the UK, with 19,495 cases reported in 2005. The danger of this infection is that if left undiagnosed, it can also cause pelvic inflammatory disease.

What are the symptoms?
A vaginal or penile discharge and a burning sensation when passing urine. Sore genital region, and sometimes a sore throat.

How is it treated?
Samples are usually taken from the genital region. If you have gonorrhoea you will be given Penicillin to treat it.

HIV and AIDS

Many people think that, because they have been hearing about HIV and AIDS for so many years, it's not a problem any more, especially if you're young and heterosexual. The reality, however, is that all sections of the population are still at risk from HIV, and 2005 saw the greatest number of new cases since the epidemic began. While gay men remain in the highest risk group for HIV transmission, heterosexual transmission of HIV has increased rapidly. During 2005 there were 3,550 reports of heterosexually acquired HIV.

What are HIV and AIDS?

HIV (Human Immunodeficiency Virus) is the virus that causes AIDS, which stands for Acquired Immunodeficiency Syndrome. HIV is a serious illness, which stops the body's immune system from fighting off disease and eventually runs the body down so that even something like the common cold becomes serious and life threatening. HIV is passed on in the sexual fluids or blood of an infected person, so if you have unprotected sex, infected blood or sexual fluid can get into your body and you can become infected. This usually happens either by having sexual intercourse with an infected person or by sharing needles used to inject drugs with an infected person. Yet another reason to use a condom and say no to drugs.

Where do I get tested and what do I do?

See your nearest GUM clinic for help. There is no cure for AIDS, though medical advances do continue for people with HIV.

Syphilis

There were 2,807 new cases of syphilis in 2005. Symptoms are usually a painless sore on or near the vagina or penis, but sometimes in the mouth or anus. This is then followed by a rash on the body and flu-like symptoms. Although syphilis is now relatively uncommon in the UK, rates have risen sharply with a 1,949 per cent increase in cases between 1996 and 2005.

Hepatitis B

This is caused by the Hepatitis B virus (HBV). HBV is much more infectious than HIV and can be transmitted through sexual contact, or contact with blood or blood-stained saliva and urine. There is no specific treatment for Hep B, but a vaccine against the virus is available at GUM clinics. Most people with Hep B recover completely after rest, but in some cases there may be long-term liver damage.

Trichomoniasis

This bacterial infection is caused by tiny parasites infecting the vagina and urethra. There were 5,638 new cases in 2005. Symptoms in women include discharge, itching and irritation, and sometimes an odd smell. Men usually have no symptoms.

Pubic lice

Also known as crabs, this is the STI most likely to make you feel horrible, simply because no-one likes to think they have small insects living on their genitals. Pubic lice are passed through sexual contact – i.e. your genitals meeting someone else's – and they are very contagious. The bad news about crabs is they can survive for twenty-four hours away from your body, so even if you are diagnosed and treated you need to wash all bedding, towels and clothing in very hot water before using them again, or else you or someone else will be re-infected. For this reason, treatment and diagnosis need to be overseen by a doctor to ensure you are 100 per cent clear.

GENITO-URINARY INFECTIONS

Genito-urinary infections are not sexually transmitted (i.e. you can just get them) but can be passed on through sex, so you need to be aware of them as well. These infections include cystitis, bladder infections, vaginal thrush and bacterial vaginosis. While many of these can be treated over the counter, it's wise not to self-diagnose. It's easy to assume a discharge is something you know, such as thrush, but beware – a discharge could be a sexually transmitted infection such as trichomoniasis. If you suspect you may be infected with anything, go to your nearest GUM clinic for a diagnosis.

Bacterial vaginosis

Bacterial vaginosis, also known as Gardenerella, is a very common bacterial infection that arises spontaneously within the body when a normal type of bacteria overgrows in the vagina. Certain things help this to happen, including douching, bubble baths and having the coil fitted. Symptoms are a bad-smelling, fishy discharge with a watery-yellow to greyish tint. Some women say it's worse after a period or having sex, and in some cases there is itching around the vulva. It's estimated that 5–30 per cent of women carry BV with no symptoms, which means this number of women could have a possible flare-up. Treatment is easy – go to your doctor's or to the GUM clinic at your local hospital and the infection will be treated with an antibiotic or with a vaginal cream.

Cystitis

Cystitis is an inflammation of the bladder, which is why sufferers always experience a frequent and painful urge to pee. It's caused by bacteria, which usually live quite happily in the bowel and anus, being spread to the urethra and bladder (often during sex, but not always). While very common, and irritating, cystitis isn't going to damage your sexual health, though it can be recurring so prevention is always the best way of dealing with it.

Avoid cystitis by:

- Going to the bathroom for a pee both before and immediately after sex. This helps flush away the bacteria that cause cystitis.
- If you're prone to attacks, avoid rough sex, or sex which involves a lot of thrusting, as this can cause small tears near the urethra and allow infection to get in and spread.
- Always make sure you're well lubricated, as lubrication will also help avoid the above.
- Make sure your boyfriend hasn't got NSU or urethritis – the male version of cystitis. Symptoms include pain on peeing and ejaculation.
- If you do get cystitis, don't just immediately go for over-the-counter medication. If it lasts more than forty-eight hours, see your doctor for antibiotics, because some bouts need stronger medication.
- During an outbreak drink plenty of water – a glass every half an hour, as it's essential you flush out the bladder.

Thrush

Thrush is a common infection caused by a fungus called *Candida albicans*. This fungus lives quite harmlessly in the digestive tract of most people, and is kept under control by 'good' bacteria in the gut. The problem with candida is, it's an opportunistic infection, which means it takes advantage of any weakness or imbalance in the body. Symptoms are extreme itchiness and a thick cottage-cheese-like discharge (very different from a normal vaginal discharge). Thrush in men usually appears as an itch around the head of the penis or under the foreskin. More severe symptoms might be red, dry, flaky patches and/or a swelling on the head of the penis.

How can you get rid of it?
Once you have been diagnosed with thrush, you can then buy an over-the-counter cream or pessary, such as Canestan (*Clotrimazole*) or Diflucan (*Fluconazole*). With anti-fungal treatment like this, thrush can be eliminated within a week. The success rate for these anti-fungal treatments is over 90 per cent, so if one cream doesn't work for you, try another.

How to prevent thrush
By far the best way to deal with thrush is prevention.

- Wear natural fibres, such as cotton, next to the genital area and avoid very tight trousers and tights as these give the fungus warm conditions for growth.
- Also avoid heavily perfumed soaps and bubble baths, as these can irritate the vaginal area. This also means not

washing your hair in the bath.

- If your thrush is recurring, always see your GP for further tests and advice.

Non-specific urethritis (NSU)

Non-specific urethritis (NSU) is an inflammation of the urethra (the tube where urine comes out) that affects men. It's also called non-gonococcal urethritis and is usually caused by having vaginal, oral or anal sex with a partner who already has a sexually transmitted infection. It's called 'non-specific' as a variety of infections can cause it. Other causes include: other genital or urinary tract infections, damage to the delicate urethra through vigorous sex. If left untreated, NSU can sometimes cause serious health problems, including inflammation of the testicles and reduced fertility.

What are the symptoms?
A white/cloudy discharge from the tip of the penis, which is often more obvious first thing in the morning. Pain, irritation or a burning sensation when passing urine and the need to pass urine often.

How is it treated?
NSU is easily treated with antibiotics, although damage to the urethra can take time to heal. Vaginal, oral and anal sex should be avoided until the treatment is completed and the infection has cleared up. To avoid re-infection, any sexual partners should also be treated.

Toxic Shock Syndrome (TSS)

Lastly, a quick word about TSS, which is not a sexually transmitted infection or caused by sex but a very rare and serious infection that's linked to tampon use, rather than caused by tampons. You will probably never get TSS or know anyone who gets it, but it's good to know what the symptoms are and how to avoid putting yourself at risk.

Bacteria called *Staphylococcus aureus* cause TSS and when a tampon is left inside your vagina for too long, it creates a perfect environment for such bacteria to grow. To avoid developing TSS, follow these guidelines when using tampons:

- Change your tampons frequently (at least every four to eight hours).
- Choose the correct tampon absorbency. Use smaller-sized tampons when your flow is lighter. TSS occurs more often when super-absorbent tampons are used. Don't use these unless your menstrual flow is extremely heavy.
- Wash your hands before inserting or taking out your tampon.
- Don't use tampons to absorb anything other than your menstrual flow. Only insert a tampon once menstrual blood is present.

If you experience the following symptoms while wearing a tampon, remove the tampon and contact your doctor. These symptoms may seem similar to those of the flu. If they occur while you are menstruating and wearing a tampon, they may signal TSS. Otherwise, they may indicate another infection.

Symptoms of TSS include:

- Sudden high fever.
- A sunburn-like rash.
- Diarrhoea.
- Dizziness, fainting or light-headedness.
- Vomiting.

THE ESSENTIAL HEALTH CHECKS

Cervical smears – all sexually active women

This is a test for all women who are having or have had sex. It's basically an internal examination whereby a nurse/doctor takes cells from the cervix in order to test for any possible changes, which could indicate pre-cancerous cells. It is not a test for cancer but to detect possible abnormalities or changes in the cells, which may develop into cervical cancer if they are not treated. If changes can be detected at an early stage, cancer can then be avoided altogether.

 The number-one risk that increases your chance of developing cervical cancer is the Human Papillomavirus (HPV) infection. Doctors believe that most women who have developed cervical cancer must have had this virus.

Is the test painful?

Smears are more uncomfortable than painful, mainly because of a device called a speculum, which is placed in the entrance of your vagina. This instrument, though torturous looking, is used simply to separate the walls of the vagina so that a doctor/nurse can literally see the condition of your cervix. A wooden spatula is then wiped across the cervix (neck of the womb) to take off cells. These cells are then smeared onto a glass slide and sent to a laboratory to be examined.

What happens after the test?

A few weeks after a smear test, your results will be sent to you. The results are likely to note one of five things:

- Inadequate – which means the nurse/doctor did not manage to pick up enough cells to get a proper report. If this happens, there is nothing to worry about and all you have to do is go back for another test.
- Negative – this gives you the all-clear and you don't have to have another test for three to five years.
- Mild dysplasia or borderline reading – this means an infection may be present and you should be screened more regularly, usually every six months.
- Moderate dysplasia – this shows inflammation in the cells and a need for more investigation.
- Severe dysplasia – means there are detectable changes in the cells and you need some treatment.

How to make the test easier

- Make an appointment with a female doctor or nurse. Even if your doctor is a man you do not have to see him for your smear but can opt for a female doctor/nurse.
- Ask the nurse/doctor to warm the speculum before it's inserted. This makes the insertion less of a shock to the system.
- Drop your tailbone. Due to nerves, many women tense before the speculum is inserted, making it more uncomfortable and difficult to adjust. One way to make insertion easier is to concentrate on dropping your tailbone (imagine the base of your spine and your bottom resting flat on the bed).
- Speak up if it's painful. Again it sounds obvious, but do speak up if it hurts because the doctor may need to use a smaller speculum.
- Avoid sex the night before you go. This is because semen makes the smear results unreliable (as does blood so avoid going when you have a period).

Cervical cancer vaccine

Cervical cancer is the second most common cancer in women under thirty-five in the UK and it claims 1,300 lives each year. The good news is that within the next five years there will be a new vaccine (Cervarix and Gardasil) that will protect you from HPV, the virus which causes cervical cancer. It will be available to all teenage girls who are not yet sexually active (after you're sexually active the vaccine won't work, as you may have HPV already).

The vaccine works by triggering the body's immune system to attack the HPV strains six and eleven, which cause genital warts and which have been linked to almost all cases of cervical cancer. However, because the vaccine protects against a sexually transmitted virus, and is given to girls at the start of puberty, some critics believe it could send a message that it's OK to have early sex. Of course this is rubbish, because while the vaccine will protect you against HPV and cervical cancer, it won't protect against pregnancy or any other STI, so basically the argument is fairly groundless.

Testicle examination – all young men

Testicular cancer is the most common cancer in men aged fifteen to thirty-four, with around 1,800 new cases diagnosed every year. The good news is that over 95 per cent of men who seek treatment in the early stages are cured. So the crucial thing is to get treatment as early as possible, meaning get to know your testicles, examine them regularly (around once a month) for what's normal and what isn't, and if you notice a change (which in most cases won't be cancer) see your doctor as soon as possible. What to look for:

- A lump in either testicle.
- Any feeling of heaviness in the scrotum.
- A dull ache in the abdomen or groin.
- A collection of fluid in the scrotum.

Breast examinations – all women

While breast cancer is virtually unheard of in people under twenty (80 per cent of breast cancers are diagnosed in women over the age of fifty), it is important to be breast aware. If you start examining your breasts when you're young, you'll get used to what's normal for you and what isn't, and you'll be able to seek help in the future if you spot anything strange. When feeling your breasts (try to do this at the same time every month, as your period will affect how your breasts feel), know what's normal for you and feel all around the breast and under it. The important thing to remember is that breasts are very lumpy when you're going through puberty, and this is normal breast tissue and nothing to be worried about. If, however, you are worried and need reassurance, see your GP.

PREGNANCY

'I've been depressed for the last couple of days about money and things like that and whether I can afford her next feed. I've been crying my eyes out. It's hard, really hard.'

DIONNE, 16, on motherhood

Think it will never happen to you? Well think again! An unplanned pregnancy will happen within a year (usually in less time than this when you're young and super-fertile) if you're having unprotected sex on a regular basis. And if you're haphazard about using contraception (such as you forget to take your pill or do nothing if a condom breaks), pregnancy is also a very real possibility.

How do I know if I am pregnant?

The most obvious sign of pregnancy is a late period. You may also notice a feeling of nausea (all day, not just in the mornings), sore breasts, excessive tiredness and the need to pee a lot; or you may not notice anything at all. So to find out for sure you always need to do a pregnancy test (sold at chemists). If you can't afford one, go to your nearest FPA/Brook clinic and they'll do one for you. These tests need to be taken once your period is late and they work by detecting pregnancy hormones present in your urine. If you do a test and it's negative and your period still doesn't come, do another test or see your GP, because you may have done the test too early.

What should I do?

If the test is positive, you now have three choices: keep the baby, have an abortion or give the baby up for adoption. This is a major decision and one that shouldn't be taken on your own no matter how old you are. As scary as it is, you need to talk to someone you trust and who you can rely on, as well as seeking the help of your GP or a doctor at a FPA or Brook clinic.

How can I tell my parents?

'I couldn't bring myself to tell my mum at first because I knew she'd go mad, and when I did she didn't speak to me for months, but then she came round and really helped me and still helps me.'

DIONNE, 16

'I was the last person to find out that Dionne was pregnant and when I did find out I was horrified, I just couldn't believe it. I can't remember what I said to her but I don't think I spoke to her for a while. I was really unhappy about it. I've got used to the idea now. I was just worried about her being sixteen and not working and with nobody to support her but she's doing well now.'

SAM, Dionne's mum

'When my parents found out she was pregnant, my step-dad went absolutely insane, saying are you ready for it and all this. Her step-dad was even worse and I got threatened to be put through a window, so that was an interesting day of my life. I know now they were just concerned about the welfare of the baby and me having a steady job, but everything has fallen into place now.'

STEVEN, 18, now father of a baby girl

Telling your parents that you are pregnant is probably number one in the Top Ten Teen Fears and the one you're probably eager never to face. However, while you can get an abortion without parental consent, most doctors will still try to persuade you to seek your parents' support; and if you are going to have the baby then you have no choice but to tell them before they spot it.

Being scared of their reaction, whether it's anger, tears or disappointment, is normal – as indeed is that reaction; however, rest assured most parents do come round and want to help, even if they lose it in the beginning. Hiding your pregnancy is just not a safe or sensible option for you or the baby, as you need medical help and support all the way through.

Plus the longer you wait to tell them, the harder it will be to explain it all later. What you need to do is pick a good time (i.e. one when no-one is rushing out of the door), and sit down and just come right out with it. You can admit you've made a mistake, ask for their help, or just say 'I don't know what to do – I'm pregnant.'

Be honest with yourself – the chances of their being over-joyed are slim to none, so don't get angry if they react badly, and remember that your own initial reaction was probably not positive either. Give them time to come round (and they will come round), and give them time to rant: the chances are that their reaction is down to worry and fear for you, rather than anger that you've let them down. What are your options now?

Abortion

An abortion or termination, as it is sometimes known, is a surgical or medical procedure that ends a pregnancy. They are legal up to twenty-four weeks, but more than 89 per cent take place within the first twelve weeks of pregnancy. An abortion must be agreed by two doctors and carried out by a doctor in a hospital or clinic. You can usually obtain the first approval from a doctor at a family-planning or young person's clinic like Brook, and most GPs will also refer for abortion. The second approval is normally given by the doctor performing the abortion. If you do not want to access an abortion through the National Health Service, you can choose to pay for one at an independent abortion clinic (such as BPAS or Marie Stopes: see Resources).

Can someone under sixteen have an abortion?

If you are under the age of sixteen you can have an abortion and give your own consent to one if a doctor agrees you are mature enough to make the decision and know what's going on. However, having said this, it is a good idea to involve your parents in your decision because it's a huge thing to go through on your own and you need someone to support and look after you post-abortion. However, if discussing it with them is out of the question or not in your best interests, another appropriate adult should be there to support you, both during and after the procedure.

Surgical abortion

The most widely used method is called vacuum aspiration – where the contents of the uterus are gently sucked away through a tube. The procedure takes about ten minutes, though you usually need to be at the clinic anywhere from two to six hours.

Early medical abortion/abortion pill

This method is usually used up to nine weeks into pregnancy, and is often known as the 'abortion pill', though this isn't very accurate as it does involve more than just taking a pill. The pills known as Mifepristone (previously RU 486) are used to cause an early miscarriage. One works by blocking the action of the hormone that makes the lining of the uterus hold onto the fertilized egg. The other, given forty-eight hours later, causes the uterus to cramp. The lining of the uterus breaks down and the embryo is lost in the bleeding that follows, as happens with a miscarriage.

The abortion pill may be an option if you:

- Are less than eight weeks pregnant.
- Are willing and able to give informed consent.
- Live no more than two hours away from emergency medical care (a hospital).
- Are able to come back to the clinic for one to three follow-up appointments.
- Agree to have a surgical abortion if the abortion pill does not induce termination.
- Are willing to insert medications into your vagina.

Should you have an abortion?

Abortion is your choice and your choice alone. It shouldn't be determined by your parents (even if you know they have your best interests at heart), by a boyfriend or by a doctor. To decide if you want one or not ask yourself:

- Will I be able to bring up a child? Think in terms of your maturity, your finances and your feelings about being a young parent.
- Could I live with having an abortion?
- What support will I get (or not) if I have this baby?
- Why do I want this child?

For more help and advice, seek the advice of someone who is fair and impartial like the British Pregnacy Advisory Service (BPAS) and Marie Stopes International. They have trained counsellors who will not make you have an abortion, will not have an agenda and will talk you through the choices of having the baby, having an abortion and adoption. Beware of pro-life campaigners and agencies (who sometimes flag themselves up as help agencies) that don't believe in abortion and may try to scare you into keeping the baby.

Adoption

If you decide adoption is the way you want to go, contact social services for advice on what help and support you will need throughout the pregnancy and they will also put you in contact with an adoption agency. It's not just a case of giving up your baby and having no say over what happens next. If you have strong feelings about what kind of family you would like to adopt your baby, discuss these with the adoption agency.

No-one decides to give a baby up for adoption lightly and it's likely you'll spend months worrying about whether you're making the right decision; this is why babies cannot be adopted until six weeks after their birth. This 'cooling-off' period is to allow you to be absolutely sure that you are making the right decision.

Keeping your baby

Many girls do, of course, keep their baby and if this is what you want to do, be sensible: seek medical help and tell your parents what's going on. Hiding it or hoping everything will work out if you ignore it is dangerous, not only for the baby's health but yours as well. There are plenty of people who can help you – social workers and health workers, as well as your parents. For more help and advice on what to do if you're pregnant contact Brook (see Resources).

YOUR QUESTIONS ANSWERED

Q About seven weeks ago I got diagnosed with chlamydia and NSU and then got it cleared up by the clinic and was told by the doctor to wait to have sex again until it had completely gone. I've been given the all-clear now, so does that mean that I am now immune to ever getting it again, and can I have unprotected sex?

A Your body doesn't build up immunity to sexually transmitted infections the way it does to some other diseases like, say, chicken pox, which means if you keep having unprotected sex you're just going to keep catching infections over and over again. With each unprotected encounter you're also increasing your risk of getting an infection that stays with you for life, such as the wart virus or herpes, and with this comes the problem of recurrent and painful flare-ups and treatment – a load of hassle that you can easily avoid by just wearing a condom when you have sex!

Q I desperately want a baby. I am fourteen and I love children and know I'd be a good mum. I feel I have a lot of love to give and think it would be great to have someone to love me completely, and my boyfriend thinks this too and promises to be a good dad. I know my mum would go mad if she knew I was planning it, but I really want to do this.

A Lots of women find they have broody feelings (a desire to have a baby) and go all doe-eyed over babies and cute children on the street. However, this is not the reality of having a baby and if that's your view you need to take a walk down to your local supermarket or park and have a look at the harassed mums and their screaming children. Having a baby is hard work and women twice your age find it really tough. Plus having a baby will not make you feel fulfilled and loved if you don't feel that already, because having a child is an overwhelming responsibility that doesn't go away even when you're tired, fed up and in need of sleep. On top of this, studies show that couples under eighteen who have a baby are three times more likely to split up – so could you be a single mum? How would you cope financially without a job and with no-one to help you? Think all this through very carefully before you do something you end up regretting.

Q My new boyfriend wants to have sex and says as he's a virgin and I am too we don't need to use condoms because he says he doesn't like them. The thing is, I've heard he's slept with quite a few girls, but I don't want to say this in case he gets annoyed with me and dumps me. How do I find out for sure?

A If you don't trust him and have a feeling he's not telling the truth, then don't even think about having sex with him. The problem is, your boyfriend seems to be contradicting himself. On the one hand he says he's a virgin but on the other he doesn't like condoms. But how does he know he doesn't like condoms if he's never had sex? Even if his comment is more of an assumption than experience, he's wrong about it being OK for virgins not to use contraception – what about protecting yourselves from pregnancy? Also, being afraid to speak up in case you get ditched is not a great sign, so you need to ask yourself if you're doing this for yourself or to keep him.

Q Last year I had an abortion and even though I know it was the right thing I feel horrible about it. I feel guilty and upset and worry constantly that I've ruined my chances of having a baby. I read somewhere that women who have abortions can't have babies because they are scarred – is this true? My mum was so angry when I was pregnant and relieved when I had an abortion, so I can't talk to her about it. Who can I turn to?

A It is extremely rare for abortions to cause fertility problems and almost all women who have had one can go on to have a baby later in life. Most women who have an abortion feel a mixture of grief, anger and misery, and this is why it's essential to talk to someone about how you feel. You may be surprised at how willing your mum is to do this. Yes, she was angry at the time, but she cares about you and wouldn't want you to be suffering like this on your own. If you really can't face talking to her, then contact Brook (see Resources) – they offer confidential post-abortion counselling.

Conclusion

WHEN I STARTED THIS TV SERIES AND THIS BOOK, I ASSUMED MY children would be educated in a biological and sexual sense at school and I would only have to give them the odd bits of advice on safe sex and things like that when they needed it. Now I realize that it's a minefield and I've got to be more up-front when they start asking questions; I've got to explain information to them in a practical way, because they may miss out on it at school or come away with the wrong information.

The confusing thing for me, and probably for you as well, is that as a parent I don't want to be permissive and I don't want to encourage my children to become sexually aware before they are ready – but when they are ready I can't put my head in the sand and pretend it's not happening. So I do have to think about this subject, I do have to be aware, I do have to be open and honest – and right from the beginning, because if I wait too long it may be too late or too difficult to get the right messages across.

The fact is, puberty, falling in love and even having sex (when they do it for the right reasons) are fantastic things – exciting, life-enhancing and for the great part good fun. And how you help your kids get through this pretty much determines how low the accompanying pain factor will be for both of you. If you give them the right tools and skills to work their way through the confusing and uncomfortable stuff, their chances of getting hurt, being broken-hearted and doing something that affects the rest of their life will be much lower. Of course, you can't save them from everything and, like most parents, no matter what I do I'm sure I'll have to put up with my fair share of vile boyfriends and mean girlfriends, clothes that shock and revolt, and even temper tantrums that will knock the wind out of me.

However – and this is a fantastically large however – the proof is out there: if you teach your kids well, they will thank you for the rest of their lives because being armed with a wealth of information about the physical and emotional parts of sex and relationships is like winning the love lottery. Not only will it help them to make decisions that are 100 per cent right, but it will also create confident and self-assured adults who are not only able to suss out the love-rats but also feel entitled to good health and happiness.

So, as embarrassing and as awkward as it is to talk to a four-year-old who is pointing at your breasts and laughing, or an eight-year-old who asks you what a blow job is, or even a fourteen-year-old who asks if you're having sex, you've got to just bite the bullet and do it. The person who's taught me the most about this is mum Kerry-Ann. She has a daughter with great self-esteem, and that's completely down to her honest and open-minded approach to sex and relationships. Even though at times her graphic approach made my toes curl, I can see that her method works. However, that doesn't mean you have to do the same: the trick with sex and relationship education is to find your own style so that you feel comfortable supplying the information and your kids feel comfortable listening to it. So use the information and techniques in this book and put your own twist on them so that, like Kerry-Ann, you can be someone with no regrets when you look back!

Appendix

SEXUAL HARASSMENT, RAPE AND CHILD ABUSE

THESE ARE ALL HORRIBLE THINGS AND HOPEFULLY YOU'LL NEVER, ever experience them, but if you do or you know someone who has been affected by any of the above, here's what you need to know:

- None of the above are ever your fault, no matter what anyone says. If someone says you were 'asking for it' or 'encouraging it' they are just trying to make you feel responsible for something they know is their fault.
- As guilty, ashamed or humiliated as you feel, always seek help if you have been affected by any of the above. If you can't tell someone you know, contact a confidential helpline who can offer you the information and support you need (Childline 0800 1111).
- Talk to someone you trust about what's happened. All of these things can cause severe trauma and suffering that can last a lifetime if you keep it to yourself. Trust

me: it wasn't your fault, no matter what you think, and there are people who can help you get over it.

- Finally, remember, your body is yours and yours alone and no-one has the right (no matter who they are – teacher, relative, boyfriend) to touch you, hurt you or abuse you in any way.

Sexual harassment

This is any kind of intentional sexual activity and touching without your consent. Under the Sexual Offences Act 2003, sexual assault includes: being made to touch any part of someone else's body, clothed or unclothed, with your body or with an object; flashing; and voyeurism.

Rape

Rape is when a person is forced into having sex. It doesn't matter if you know the person, have been on a date with the person, or even if you have been seeing each other for quite a while – being forced to have sex, either physically (being held down) or verbally (being threatened), is still rape.

Child abuse

This is when an adult, relative or older person attacks you in a physical, verbal or sexual way. Incest is when a child is sexually abused by a member of their immediate family.

HELP, ADVICE AND SUPPORT

- **Childline**
  45 Folgate Street
  London
  E1 6GL
  Confidential helpline – 0800 1111
  www.childline.org.uk

  Help and advice for children who are in distress. Childline is soon to become part of the NSPCC.

- **Rape Crisis Federation**
  www.rapecrisis.co.uk

  Gives advice and information and will refer you to your nearest rape crisis centre.

- **NSPCC**
  Helpline – 0808 800 5000
  www.nspcc.org.uk

  Helpline for anyone concerned about a young person at risk of ill-treatment or abuse.

- **Victim Support**
  0845 30 30 900
  www.victimsupport.org.uk

  Victim Support helps people to cope with the effects of any crime and provides free and confidential support and information.

- **Women's Aid**
  0808 2000247
  www.womensaid.org.uk

  National domestic violence helpline and website offering advice and help, as well as legal support to anyone who needs it.

Resources

SEX AND RELATIONSHIP RESOURCES

- **Sex Education Forum**
  National Children's Bureau
  Information line – 020 7843 1901
  www.ncb.org.uk/sef

  The national forum on sex and relationship education with a fantastic range of publications and fact sheets to help provide information and support to anyone wanting to teach SRE in the home or at school.

- **Avert**
  www.avert.org

  An international AIDS and HIV charity with an excellent website with information and advice on sex, sex education, STIs and contraception.

- **Body and Soul**
  020 7383 7678
  www.bodyandsoul.demon.co.uk

  A UK charity supporting children, teenagers, women, heterosexual men and their families who are living with or closely affected by HIV and AIDS

- **British Pregnancy Advisory Service (BPAS)**
  Head Office
  Austy Manor
  Stratford Road
  Wootton Wawen
  Henley in Arden
  B95 6BX
  Confidential helpline – 0845 730 4030
  www.bpas.org

  BPAS is the leading provider of abortion services in the UK. The site provides information, help and services relating to abortion.

- **Brook Advisory Centres**
  421 Highgate Studios
  53–79 Highgate Road
  London
  NW5 1TL
  Confidential helpline – 0800 0185 023
  www.brook.org.uk

  Brook provides free and confidential sexual-health advice and contraception to young people up to the age of twenty-five.

- **FPA (formerly the Family Planning Association)**
  2–12 Pentonville Road
  London
  N1 9FP
  Confidential helpline – 0845 310 1334
  www.fpa.org.uk

  Wide-ranging advice on contraception, sexual health and pregnancy.

- **London Lesbian and Gay Switchboard**
  Confidential helpline – 020 7837 7324
  www.llgs.org.uk (for regional switchboards)

  The switchboard aims to provide an information, support and referral service for anyone worried about their sexuality, as well as for lesbians, gay men and bisexual people throughout the UK.

- **Marie Stopes International**
  153–157 Cleveland Street
  London
  W1T 6QW
  Confidential helpline – 0845 300 8090
  www.mariestopes.org.uk

- **Like it is – Marie Stopes teen advice**
  www.likeitis.org

  Advice on contraception, sexual health, abortion, pregnancy and where to find the nearest Marie Stopes Clinic.

- **LifeBytes**
  www.lifebytes.gov.uk

  Website aimed at eleven- to fourteen-year-olds giving information and advice on a range of issues, including drugs, alcohol, sex and relationships.

- **National Sexual Health Line**
  Confidential helpline – 0800 567 123

  Gives confidential advice and information about HIV, AIDS and STIs.

- **Parentline Plus**
  Helpline – 0800 800 2222
  www.parentlineplus.org.uk

  Support on all issues related to parenting a child.

- **Sex, Etc.**
  www.sxetc.org

  US sex and relationships website run by teens for teens.

- **Sexwise**
  Confidential helpline – 0800 28 29 30 (7am–midnight)
  www.ruthinking.co.uk

  Information and guidance to young people under eighteen about sex, relationships and contraception. The website also helps you search for services anywhere in the UK.

- **Teenage Health Freak**
  www.teenagehealthfreak.org

  An excellent website for teenagers, including a place to email your questions.

- **The Site**
  www.thesite.org.uk

  The Site provides fantastic fact sheets and articles on all the key issues facing young people, including: sex and relationships; drinking and drugs; work and study; housing, legal and financial issues; and health and well-being.

TESTICULAR CANCER

- **CancerBACUP**
  0808 800 1234
  www.cancerbacup.org.uk

  Europe's leading cancer information service, with over 4,500 pages of up-to-date cancer information, practical advice and support for cancer patients, their families and carers.

- **Cancer Research UK**
  PO Box 123
  Lincoln's Inn Fields
  London
  WC2A 3PX
  020 7242 0200
  www.cancerresearchuk.org

  Site for the Cancer Research charity, giving information on cancer, the latest news and research findings relating to various types of cancer, and information on where to go for help and advice.

- **The Testicular Cancer Resource Centre**
  http://tcrc.acor.org

  A site offering information on testicular cancer.

- **Testicular Cancer UK**
  www.checkemlads.com

  A site offering information on testicular cancer.

GENERAL ADVICE RESOURCES

- **ABC – Anti-Bullying Campaign**
  www.bullying.co.uk

  A comprehensive website aimed at helping young people suffering from bullying. It covers the various forms that bullying can take and the places it may happen. It gives information, advice and tips to parents, teachers, health workers and other people trying to support victims of bullying. This includes legal advice, government advice to LEAs and schools, projects that are currently running in schools and advice on how to compose correspondence, and much else. There is an email address you can write to for advice and help, from which you should receive a reply within 24 hours – help@bullying.co.uk

- **Acne Support Group**
  PO Box 9
  Newquay
  Cornwall
  TR9 6WG
  0870 870 2263
  www.stopspots.org

  Provides support and advice for those who suffer from spots or acne. The website offers information about what causes the condition and how best to treat it.

- **Adfam**
  Waterbridge House
  32–36 Loman Street
  London
  SE1 0EH
  020 7928 8898
  admin@adfam.org.uk

Adfam offers support to families who have a member facing problems with alcohol or drug abuse.

- **Alcohol Concern**
  Waterbridge House
  32–36 Loman Street
  London
  SE1 0EE
  020 7928 7377
  www.alcoholconcern.org.uk

  This is a body made up of 500 local agencies who are involved in promoting alcohol issues in government, and offers an information service on where to go for help, factual information on alcohol and related problems such as abuse, and information on events and training for those supporting people with alcohol issues.

- **Alcoholics Anonymous**
  www.alcoholics-anonymous.org.uk
  National helpline – 0845 769 7555

  A support group run by alcoholics for alcoholics.

- **Al-Anon and Alateen**
  Al-Anon Family Groups UK & Eire
  61 Great Dover Street
  London
  SE1 4YF
  020 7403 0888
  www.al-anonuk.org.uk

  Al-Anon offers understanding and support for families and friends of problem drinkers, whether the alcoholic is still drinking or not. Alateen is a part of Al-Anon and is for young people aged from twelve to twenty who have been affected by someone else's drinking, usually that of a parent.

- **British Association for Counselling and Psychotherapy**
  BACP House
  35–37 Albert Street
  Rugby
  Warwickshire
  CV21 2SG
  0870 443 5252
  www.bacp.co.uk

  The official site for the British Association for Counselling and Psychotherapy, offering a listing of therapists and a link to help the general public find a recognized therapist in their area.

- **British Nutrition Foundation**
  High Holborn House
  52–54 High Holborn
  London
  WC1V 6RQ
  020 7404 6504
  www.nutrition.org.uk

  Offering information on nutrition and health, food commodities, food labelling and how to find a dietician or nutritionist.

- **Depression Alliance**
  212 Spitfire Studios
  63–71 Collier Street
  London
  N1 9BE
  0845 123 23 20
  www.depressionalliance.org

  The site provides information and support for people suffering from depression. The Depression Alliance campaign aims to raise awareness amongst the general public about the realities of depression.

- **Drinkline**
  Confidential helpline – 0800 917 82 82

  Help for people suffering from the results of alcohol abuse.

- **Eating Disorders Association**
  103 Prince of Wales Road
  Norwich
  NR1 1DW
  Confidential youth helpline – 0845 634 7650
  www.edauk.com

  The site provides information and help on all aspects of eating disorders, including anorexia nervosa, bulimia nervosa, binge eating disorder and related eating disorders.

- **Mind**
  15–19 Broadway
  London
  E15 4BQ
  Information line – 0845 766 0163
  www.mind.org.uk

  Mind is a mental health charity, and the site provides information on mental health issues and problems, and where to go for help.

- **Narcotics Anonymous**
  www.ukna.org
  UK helpline – 0845 3733366

  A support group run by recovering addicts for anyone affected by drugs.

- **National Association for Pre-menstrual Syndrome**
  NAPS
  41 Old Road
  East Peckham
  Kent
  TN12 5AP
  0870 777 2177
  www.pms.org.uk

  NAPS advice is prepared by clinicians and expert patient members to help all those affected by PMS and menstrual ill-health. The site provides information on the psychological, behavioural and physical effects of PMS, ways of dealing with those effects, diet advice and expert advice.

- **National Centre for Eating Disorders**
  54 New Road
  Esher
  Surrey
  KT10 9NU
  0845 838 2040
  www.eating-disorders.org.uk

  National Centre for Eating Disorders is an independent organization set up to provide solutions for all eating problems, compulsive or 'binge' eating, failed or 'yo-yo' dieting, bulimia and anorexia. The site provides information on these issues, counselling services and help from experts.

- **Netdoctor**
  www.netdoctor.co.uk

  An independent UK health website with great factsheets and information written by medical professionals.

- **NHS Direct**
  0845 4647
  www.nhsdirect.nhs.uk

  Provides information on NHS services and how to find your local doctor, dentist, optician or pharmacy.

- **NO Panic**
  Helpline – 0808 808 0545 (freephone) or
  01952 590 545

  A site offering support to those suffering from panic attacks, phobias, obsessive compulsive disorder, general anxiety disorders.

- **Quitline**
  0800 00 22 00
  www.quit.org.uk

  Helpline for those trying to give up smoking.

- **Re-Solv**
  Helpline – 0808 800 2345
  www.re-solv.org

  Helpline for those wishing to give up solvent abuse.

- **Samaritans**
  National helpline – 08457 90 90 90
  www.samaritans.org

  Helpline for people in crisis, despairing or suicidal. You can speak in total confidence with a volunteer about anything that is troubling you.

- **Stress**
  www.stress.org.uk

  The site gives information on stress and how to manage it and the issues relating to stress.

- **Talk to Frank**
  Confidential helpline – 0800 77 66 00
  www.talktofrank.com

  The site provides information on drugs, addiction, issues relating to both and where to go for help.

Index